dialogue with death

dialogue with death

abraham schmitt

WORD BOOKS, Publisher

Waco, Texas

ISBN 0–87680–454–7
Library of Congress catalog card number: 76–1731
Printed in the United States of America

acknowledgments

A special acknowledgment goes to the many people—the dying, the survivors, and the living—who talked with me about death. The courageous ones who spoke in my classes and seminars when death was imminent deserve a special thanks. I wish also to recognize here the many people who so gladly shared their journals or their confrontation with death which became a major portion of the text of this book. Their names or pseudo-names appear in the pages that follow.

Two people deserve my gratitude for their part in the writing of this book: Ronald Yoder, of Choice Books, Harrisonburg, Virginia, conceptualized a publication like this after hearing a chapel address on death given by me at Eastern Mennonite College and encouraged me to undertake such a venture. My wife, Dorothy, edited and typed and retyped the entire text. I especially appreciated that she, as a registered nurse, inspired my dialogue with death even as she participated in the confrontation and resolution of the many issues raised.

contents

introduction

There is no escape from death, but modern man has done all he can to avoid death, to delay it, and to evade all thoughts and conversations about it. Like the subject of sex in former generations, it is a taboo.

The most tragic result is that to deny death is to forfeit life also since death and life are so interrelated. Death is merely the end of finite existence. To live life fully, one must yield to the limits that this finiteness imposes. To face finiteness at any one moment is to touch immediately ultimate finiteness, namely, death. But the opposite is also true: To come to terms with death opens life up to new dimensions. Or, as Feifel has said, "Life is not genuinely our own until we can renounce it." To have dialogue with death until we renounce life so as to genuinely live it to its fullest is the intent of this book.

My hope is that the reader will join hands with me, as hundreds if not thousands of people have already done, and come walk with death. Dare to do it, and then dare to live the new life that this release will give you.

People often ask me, "How can you continue this preoccupation with death? Isn't it morbid?" Far from it. I am just as much preoccupied with life. I am much more prone to overwhelm my colleagues with my optimism—by my excitement and enthusiasm with life. In fact, dealing with death

9

became a gateway to a new land that often takes on Edenic attributes.

I must admit that at times I don't want to get more and more involved in the subject of death. But each time I do, the reward for having risked again far outweighs the cost.

After the third year of teaching the course on death and dying at the University of Pennsylvania, I wanted to take a break. Then one day I got a call from the dean saying that a petition had been received from students demanding that the course be taught. I remember my instantaneous but so appropriate response, "Oh, grief!" But that year, with sixty-four students enrolled in courses, proved to be the highlight. Many of the journal entries included in later chapters come from these classes.

Only today I finished writing the final chapter. I then volunteered to do any menial task that I could for the family simply to escape the subject matter of death. There is a time to forget the subject too!

In the waiting room of a music studio I made idle conversation with a mother who was also there with a child taking lessons. She casually mentioned her brother-in-law who had only a year ago returned from a three-year rendezvous with death. I stopped her long enough to get a pad and pencil and her permission to copy her statements. Here they are:

He appreciates life like none of us do because it was nearly taken from him. He knows what life is all about because he had to think so much what it would be like without it. He notices the little things that we take for granted. He marvels at the beauty of the sky when we forget to look. Even my smile now means so much to him, and I don't know I'm smiling. You only need to shake hands with him and he knows your feelings. When he looks into your eyes, he sees your whole inside. He sees your soul! The smallest things we do for him he appreciates. He makes the little things big. Just to be with him makes everyone more alive. You begin to notice what he notices, see what he sees. They were always there, but you didn't care. He makes you see beauty everywhere. I have never experienced anyone so close to death who came back so alive.

My immediate response—"This is exactly the subject of my book." One more occasion to dialogue with death and I come back more alive. This book will provide an endless stream of conversations. It is a contagious process to free people to face their worst fear and then in gratitude infect others with a newly won freedom.

It is not my intent to answer a lot of questions or to deal with all the ethical issues that the subject of death arouses. I have deliberately avoided doing this because even that can be a very comfortable way of evading the subject. I do not wish to participate further in such an intellectualization-rationalization process. In selecting quotations, I always gave preference to those that grappled with gut feelings in lieu of profound explanations.

It will also be very apparent that the spiritual dimensions of life and death are frequently included. I do not apologize for this because I am deeply committed to a Judeo-Christian faith and its meaning for mortal as well as immortal existence. There is no intent on my part to impose this upon the reader. As best I could, I allowed the persons I quote to describe and define their own position. However, it was no surprise to me when the whole spiritual dimension of the subject was frequently freely shared in class as well as in the journals.

The inspiration and the material for this book come out of a five-year teaching venture on the subject of death and dying. I had a growing yearning to do this when I noticed that more and more public awareness of death was surfacing on many fronts. The popular journals, both professional and lay, were the first to respond. Then came a multitude of scholarly textbooks and personal autobiographies. I believed that four professional groups should get involved because they are all directly concerned in the dying process: medicine, social work, divinity, and nursing. I invited all of these departments to join me in offering an interdisciplinary graduate seminar on death and dying at the University of Pennsylvania where I held an assistant professorship. I also taught the class in the undergraduate school of the same university, in church settings, in social welfare agencies, in seminaries, and at pastoral institutes.

Three keys to success in teaching so vulnerable a subject were: firsthand confrontation by all students of as many dying people, films, and scenes as possible; an immediate processing of all the feelings in a group setting; and the most important tool—the "Death and Dying Journal." Every student was expected to keep a weekly log of his or her inner conversation with death.

These journals became the major source of quotations for this book. I have used this material with students' permission, but it is also disguised so as to conceal identity. In describing dying guests, identity and identifying data are changed so that no one may recognize them.

Only Uncle Bill in the first chapter is not disguised. However, I have informed his family of my use of this experience with him. In a sense I really did get permission before he died because we both lamented the fact that I had failed to bring my tape recorder to keep his spoken word permanently. I know he would want me to use the experience the way I did in this book.

The book begins and ends with accounts of death. Both accounts are very dramatic because these two people were articulate and there was someone ready to hear them tell it. Both individuals died only days later.

In chapter 2, I felt a need to tell my own life's journey with death. These experiences with death are not the usual and may account for the fact that I got enthralled enough with death to write this book. I believe the reader needs to meet me.

The following two chapters (3 and 4) focus on teaching death and dying courses. The first uses a student journal to show how near death is at all times. It may be a parent of a student who dies while the course is in session, or even a student coping with her own illness, as is the case of Wendy M. After completing this chapter, I sent it to her for approval. Instead of returning it by mail, she brought it to me in person for two reasons: her kidney problem is very real with the prognosis unknown; death was so real a possibility that she was unable to continue her journal. She also requested that her first name be used. This she dramatically acted out by signing my manuscript with Wendy M. If she should in fact die, she would want this chapter to tell correctly how vividly she lived with death. Chapter 4 continues the same theme of student reactions in their encounter with death.

Illustrations such as chapter 5 are becoming more and more plentiful. People who have personally confronted death have returned from it full of vitality for living an effective life thereafter. The purpose of this chapter is to raise the prime question of the whole book. Is it possible to confront one's own death vicariously and then return to a new, victorious, fulfilling life without having an encounter with one's real death?

Suicide is a difficult subject. Since I as the death educator had an experience with it, I have included it as chapter 6.

Chapters 7 and 8 deal with grief. The grieving can teach us a lot about death because they are so close to it. It is my hope that this book will encourage many of us to extend ourselves to those in sorrow and say, "Tell me all about it," and then hold dear what they say.

Chapter 9 takes us on a personal journey of death with a brilliant, articulate scholar who comes to a simple conclusion.

Sheila Scott (not her real name) is a young student who had a real-life encounter with death. A small portion of her journal comprises chapter 10.

Some people can let go of life when it is finished. Others need our help during those final moments. After we begin dialogue with our own death, we need to be available to others to be that last link with life for them. Then when our day comes, hopefully there will be people available and prepared to do it for us. Chapter 11 illustrates this area of helping.

Chapter 12 is my personal hope for dealing with death in the future. I long for a better day for death.

Then finally we all must take that incredible journey as chapter 13 describes. Maybe it won't be as frightening as we always thought.

And so now come join me in your dialogue with death, even as I am dialoguing. And then reach out to someone else who needs to dialogue. It is contagious!

1

o grave,
where is thy victory?

Uncle Bill! Why did you have to die? You were so young—
only forty-nine years of age and far younger in body and
heart. And that awful disease—ALS—that horrible disease!
Why that disease? Then again, it would take a brutal disease
to slay you. But why you? You had so young a wife who
needed you so desperately, not to mention your four children,
especially the two young fellows. They above all others needed
a father like you for at least eight years longer. The one with
the cleft palate needed corrective surgery. Emotionally he
needed a strong father standing by. But you are gone!

It's almost unbearable to think that suffering has been your
companion before. The bride of your youth died only a few
years after the wedding. Is there no justice in matters like
this?

Uncle Bill, your death was phenomenal. It's hard to think
that you died at all. You ascended! You were simply transformed to your celestial body after your earthly body crum-
bled away—it can't be any other way. You departed so
gloriously and triumphantly. By all earthly standards your
death was cruel and murderous; yet the more viciously the

horrible disease ravaged your body, the more victoriously you
ascended to higher and higher plains. At last the final step
was taken from the highest cloud to the realms beyond. Without a shadow of doubt, in your mind Jesus was standing
there, extending his hand and saying, "Well done, my loyal
and faithful servant."

Four years ago I first heard from my family in faraway
western Canada that Uncle Bill was fatally ill. They couldn't
say the name of the disease. "It goes by several letters. He has
only two years to live. . . . He wants to see you. He wants
you to come home. Please hurry!"

But how could I? I was three thousand miles away in a
complicated life—four children of our own, a family to provide for, a university commitment. The faint plea never left
me. I should go!

At the time I was well into my academic journey with
"Death and Dying." The course had already proved a phenomenal success, oversubscribed by graduate students, a sell-
out. I received a steady stream of affirmation. "Oh, by the
way, Dr. Schmitt, my advisee tells me your class is the best
thing that ever happened to him." Or, "Say, Professor, you
really handled that dying guest in class with profound skill!"
An expert on death, they called me. But what about Uncle
Bill?

A fellow professor was dying of the same disease. Each
semester he gladly came to class, and toward the end of the
course, we all went to his house to hear him describe his journey toward the grave. His rapidly deteriorating body was a
vivid reminder of how fast two years vanish. Looking past
his wheelchair, I always saw Uncle Bill, not my colleague,
and heard the ebbing cry, "Come home."

The summer of 1972 was exactly right to make the long
trek back "home." Often, as we passed familiar landmarks
en route, the fleeting thought crossed my mind, "Is he still
alive?" Half of me was yearning to see him; the other half

recoiled at the nagging thought of what might be expected of me. I might have been teaching a course on death, but that didn't mean I performed miracles. To underscore my frailty, I always begin my first class with the statement, "I am a dying professor, teaching a group of dying graduate students about death." That didn't sound very helpful for a dying person.

We had no sooner arrived at Swift Current when scores of relatives proclaimed, "Uncle Bill is waiting for you. He will not last long. He can receive visitors for only twenty minutes at a time. You must go to Medicine Hat, Alberta, immediately. . . . Oh, by the way, don't call ahead because the anticipation of visitors is too much for him to bear."

They had all been down to see him repeatedly. Although it was nearly two hundred miles away, some cited as many as a dozen visits during the past two years. What made visiting him so special? From all I had experienced, most dying were shunned!

Uncle Bill had a very special place in my life. He was only a few years older than I. We grew up across the street from each other in that little prairie village with the beautiful German name "Blumenort." He was my ideal, the ideal of most village boys—the great ball player who hit the homerun of the season to win the famous pennant for our village. He was a skilled craftsman in metal and in wood, with the perfect physique. What more does a teenager ask of life?

Then he "became a Christian" and lived that life like he played ball. Everybody knew it immediately. He went along the pathways and highways proclaiming his new Companion with vigor and enthusiasm. Watching him left so deep an impression on me that I found no peace until I followed him as he followed Christ.

When he began a second courtship, I was old enough to join him in double dating. This girl became his second bride and the mother of his four children.

After this, I lost track of him. I vanished in the world of the American college and university.

Now—twenty years later—he was calling me and he was dying.

That mysterious, fatal disease has by now become a familiar companion of mine. ALS, amyotrophic lateral sclerosis, was Lou Gehrig's disease. The great New York Yankee slugger—493 home runs to be exact, the Iron Horse who played 2,130 straight games—was leveled by ALS right at his famous first-base position during the 1939 season. I love him most of all for the way he wept before a record crowd that gave him a standing ovation when he officially retired to die.

From the first symptom, this disease wages a hellish war on the entire muscular system. It literally atrophies and then petrifies every muscle in the body, beginning with the extremities, on to the vital organs. At first it causes weakness of arms and legs, then paralysis of the entire body, and finally death. All this is accomplished in an orderly way with a time schedule of almost exactly two years. What makes it so devilish a disease is that the mind is never affected; its victim is perfectly able to watch himself die, bit by bit. Yet one does not know exactly which vital organ may be suddenly affected thus causing instant death. During the entire time, everyone knows it is incurable and irreversible. It is like condensing the aging process at an incredible pace for one person while all the rest are tuned in on natural time. Maybe an even more gruesome comparison is to be under a guillotine blade that is programmed to drop at any unknown time within a two-year span.

How anyone could endure it was beyond me to imagine. At least so I thought before I met Uncle Bill.

We are coming, Uncle Bill! The straight 150-mile Highway 1 gave me ample time to meditate. What would he be like? What should I say? How do you greet so close a relative, whom you haven't seen in adult life, when in fact you ought to say good-bye forever to him?

It was confusing! Sure I had been teaching course after course on death and dying, but there are no tricks to learn in this trade. It all seemed to no avail.

With remarkable professional sensitivity and courage, I had gone to many strangers' bedsides and extended my hand to them so that they could unburden their final struggle. I had even brought these patients to class and done a model interview for my students, but I had never met with anyone so close to me who was dying. It had never been Uncle Bill.

Several times I caught myself sinking my fingernails into the palms of my hands as I clutched the motionless steering wheel. Gee, was I tense!

We did stop in a little dusty prairie ranching town to call ahead to make sure all was well for our visit. Christine, his beautiful wife, left no doubt on that score as she exclaimed, "Come, come. By all means come. Bill is waiting. Not a day has gone by without your name being mentioned." I asked how long we should expect to stay. "Never mind—just come. He is going on pure oxygen now, and he will be ready when you get here."

Before we knew it, we were suddenly there, no more struggling with proper etiquette. There he stood in front of me near the door, waiting. Those same blue eyes, glittering with fiery determination like they always had, but what an emaciated body! His feet were set far apart to give more balance. I took his rigid hand, which was cold and felt like that of a skeleton. *"Auschwitz,"* I breathed to myself.

In a gush of excitement, I exclaimed, "Bill, why are you standing here—shouldn't you be in bed?"

Bill replied in old familiar language, "Oh! Brother, my brother in Christ. The Lord has provided that we shall meet before I go. You don't know how grateful I am to see you. I wanted to see you like no one else. Come, let us talk."

Inside I was relieved that the fact of death was in no way hidden. He knew he was dying, and we were going to talk about it!

Christine, in her strained cheerfulness, lovingly commented, "In no way would he stay in bed. He has waited too long. He spent the time since you called inhaling oxygen so he would have the energy he needed for this visit."

Struggling toward the sofa in two-inch sliding steps, Bill maneuvered his body to the right spot and suddenly let it drop with the same precision by which he had always lived. Then he remarked, "I don't want people to help me. They just throw me off balance."

At first he wanted to know all about us, question after question in quick succession. Every second had to be utilized to the fullest. "Where have you been? What are you doing? How is teaching in the university? How has it been between the Lord and you?"

Then came the lead question, "Say! I understand you teach a course about death. What do you teach?"

I assured him that I had no great wisdom on the subject— that he would be far more capable of teaching it than I, that I would really love to have him come to my class and tell them what he had experienced, for that was exactly where we got our material from dying guests. That made him the expert. He waved that idea aside, but the fact that a prime resource patient had ALS fascinated him. We began comparing notes. Soon he was turned on to tell me about his fight with that "torturous killer." I moved much closer to him. We faced each other directly, with eyes interlocking, as he told of his two-year struggle, detail by detail. He carefully monitored my fascination, which I underscored with many affirming remarks, such as: "Oh, how awful! How could you take it?" The account began with one very strange twitch in his arm, followed by a weakening of that arm—then the diagnosis. He commented, "It strikes only one person per million; so in all of Canada there could only be twenty-two people with this disease." The reorientation of the entire family was excruciatingly painful. The breadwinner, the family hero, the axis around whom the family rotated, rapidly disintegrated, and death was imminent.

At this point I asked him specifically, "Bill! Why are you full of excitement when most people are so frightened of death?"

He was ready for that question. "My life is in Jesus' hands. Even when this withered body gives out on me, I will live." Then he began quoting Scripture verse after Scripture verse, sometimes whole chapters, from memory. All of them proclaimed clearly and without a shadow of a doubt that he was heaven-bound to be with "my Jesus." And he stood on the threshold at this moment!

When he quoted Scripture, his face took on a glowing countenance as his fiery eyes glittered like an old-fashioned revival preacher. I can still see him staring at the ceiling as he spun off Jesus' words:

Let not your heart be troubled: ye believe in God, believe also in me. In my Father's house are many mansions: if it were not so, I would have told you. I go to prepare a place for you. And if I go and prepare a place for you, I will come again, and receive you unto myself; that where I am, there ye may be also. And whither I go ye know, and the way ye know (John 14:1–4).

"Then there is a verse in Romans that is especially meaningful to me. It has to do with the redemption of the body. Now, let me see. It's in chapter . . . what's wrong with me? I can't think of it. I knew it only yesterday, and it's my favorite." He became desperate. Racking his mind did no good. Big tears formed in his eyes and rolled down his face. I became overwhelmed and choked up too and began blowing my nose. We were both so painfully aware that he was failing rapidly.

"I'm forgetting more and more. I used to be able to recite any verse I wanted to. Can you help me? It's in the Book of Romans. It's a promise about a renewed body."

I told him that I didn't know, that I never memorized the Bible like he did, and I was sorry I could not help him.

Christine couldn't think of it either. It was so important to him. He wanted to make a point, but he couldn't. He kept on struggling and struggling, muttering phrases and words, trying to put words together. This man was bringing his life to a closure, and the end was very near. He knew it.

Finally he asked for his Bible, and I took it to him. He couldn't hold or turn the pages of the beat-up, worn-out book. The New Testament was dog-eared and finger-marked. Verse after verse was underlined with pencil and different colored pens. The margins were full of markings.

Then he instructed me to open to Romans and turn the pages. Only a glance at the page and he said, "Next, next." He didn't have to read it; he recognized each page.

"Stop! There it is!" he said with the excitement of a gold miner finding a huge nugget. His eyes glowed as he read the verse, repeating the words: ". . . even we ourselves groan within ourselves, waiting for the adoption, to wit, the redemption of our body" (Rom. 8:23).

As Bill talked about the new body he was expecting to get immediately upon death, I moaned inwardly, "Oh! Bill, you deserve it so much. This body has been cruel to you."

After one hour I began to declare that we had better leave, but to no avail. Christine insisted, "No, no, just stay. Nothing is too much for him. Being alone by himself is far worse. He has been waiting for months and months for this time. This is his finest hour. He hasn't been this alert for a long time. When he has had too much, he falls asleep. But not this! He needs you to stay."

Nonetheless, he needed oxygen. So, with some help, he was up on his feet and shuffling toward the bedroom.

In about ten minutes he came back. "Good as new," he pronounced with an impish look on his face.

For another hour we reviewed our entire past—our childhood together, the years of double dating, the many years apart. We clearly told each other how much we each had meant to the other, especially at several key crisis points.

I looked over to his wife and the three children who were in the room. Even though grief and exhaustion encircled their eyes, the glow of the present profoundly beautiful experience shone through their faces. He was saying good-bye in an intensely meaningful way. We had just underscored the landmarks of this life he had lived. Beyond any doubt, he knew where his next life would be. I couldn't help but see him walking up to Jesus with a new body replacing this shriveled-up one, extending his hand with a gush of excitement, "It's me, Bill. I have come home," and Jesus responding, "Welcome, Bill, my good and faithful servant. You have fought a good fight, you have kept the faith, and now here is your inheritance that was laid away for you from the beginning of time."

Another hour passed, and we prepared to leave. How do you say good-bye to a dying friend? I don't know. There was no use kidding anyone with, "We'll see you," or, "Oh, you'll be all right," because those words are lies and masks to cover the unbearable truth.

I thought of embracing him, but how do you embrace a skeleton? I couldn't do it. So we clasped hands and silently looked at each other as tears welled up. Then I said, "Good-bye, Bill."

But he added, "We *will* see each other again." As he underscored *will,* we both knew it was not on this earth. In less than a week he was dead.

No, Bill, you didn't simply die! You went blazing out of

this life like Ben Hur on his chariot. Your life gained momentum as your time was running out, until the final centrif-
ugal force sent you into the blue yonder.

Pascal has said, "It's not death I fear but dying." Maybe he
didn't know how to die. Maybe Uncle Bill could have shown
him the way.

Hundreds of people came from great distances to the funeral.
"Why," I kept on asking myself, "would a mob of people
pack a church for the burial of a simple laborer? Sure, I
understand when it's a dignitary, a president, or the like. But
why for you, Uncle Bill?"

After the service, the large flock milled about slowly outside. It was the strangest sensation. No one appeared sure
whether to cry profusely or rejoice ecstatically. It was like
the beautiful aftermath of the soaking rain on the parched
Alberta prairie. I had the distinct impression that most of his
relatives felt that they would gladly trade places with Bill if
they could go like he did.

It makes sense now—all the pilgrimages these people made
to his bedside. They were overwhelmed by the power that
carried this man to the grave and beyond. They had come to
learn to die, and now the lesson was over!

As people left for the long trek home, I am sure one
thought lingered: Now that I am alive, but will die, what am
I going to do with my life? I have it to live now. I must make
it count. Then when my time comes, maybe I can end it
triumphantly like he did.

Our family left the funeral and "home" to tour the Canadian
Rockies. The sights were magnificent, far beyond my greatest
imagination. A strange peace came over all of us in the presence of the gorgeous towering mountains.

One evening after one more tour of the mountains as far
north as the ice fields, I went to be alone just below the painted
peaks known as Three Sisters. As I sat on a log at nightfall,
I was entranced by the grandiose sight. When I attempted to

comprehend the glory of the moment, suddenly the words "Uncle Bill" crossed my mind:

Yes, Bill, this you have done for me. You have in your death added a dimension to life that I could never have reached on my own. The scene I now see is but symbolic of the inner glow that I now experience for having dared to walk to the grave with you. Then why do we fear the dying?

In my rapturous gaze, suddenly the mountain peak was transformed into an emaciated arm and a crooked finger, straining to point upward. The gorgeous blue of the sky became those piercing blue eyes. And I heard the words, "Behold, I go . . ."

Yes, Bill! Beyond all this beauty there is a greater glory. What I now sense is magnificent, but it is not the end. It is deliberately meant to be to give us a foretaste of what is yet to come so we will long for more.

Why did you, Uncle Bill, die? Maybe that is the wrong question to ask. Job was told to ask *how,* not *why.*

There were hundreds, if not thousands, monitoring your dying. And in doing it, we all collided with our death and our finiteness. We were made to face, even against our wishes, that we are victims of our humanity. We are time-bound beings, and time is limited. Three score and ten, or is it only two score and nine?

Thanks, Uncle Bill, for telling us.

2

my dialogue with death

Oh, death! Why am I so enthralled with you? Why have I been fascinated with you all my life? Why was I so captivated by you that I have spent all this time observing you? Do I not fear you like everyone else? Or do I fear you so much that all this confrontation is my desperate effort to make peace with death?

I am in the middle-age phase of life, which means I could expect to live again as long as I already have. I am, to the best of my knowledge, in good health, with no known illness. No one has died in my immediate family. My parents are alive and well, and even one of my grandmothers. So why this rendezvous with death that has involved literally thousands of other people?

For the past five years I have made the study, the teaching, lecturing on, and therapy of the dying and grieving a major portion of my life. At times I have been totally immersed in the subject. Why?

Five years ago, when I first proposed to teach a course on death and dying in the graduate schools of the University of

Pennsylvania, I startled my professor colleagues. Why teach such a course when issues of social change for the living were a far more pressing concern? No one had mentioned the need for this course, but an inner compulsion kept pushing me on. There were frequent puns in staff meetings that brought snickers and at times an uproar of laughter. "Gallows humor," I muttered to myself and kept on pursuing the course. On other more formal occasions when faculty approval had to be given, a very noticeable discomfort was present when even the course title had to be mentioned. It was much more consoling to everyone when I finally changed the course title to "D and D." I kept on asking myself, "Why do I have to do it?" I even wondered if there was something wrong with me.

My students had to face the same confrontation. One student made the following journal entry:

This evening my wife jokingly asked, "How's that 'dead' course coming?" I tried to explain to her the little bit that I actually knew about the course. Throughout our discussion she just kept shaking her head. "I can't see why you'd want a course like death and dying," she exclaimed. "Your prof must be some kind of a weird guy," she continued. I didn't really have much response for her. Maybe I am crazy to take such a course, but I'm going to stick with it. We'll see what happens.

As a psychotherapist, I am well aware that something out of my dim past may be affecting me now. I did have several very real encounters with death. Maybe therein lies the answer to my curiosity about the subject known to be man's ultimate enemy. But then again—maybe not.

The moment of my birth was very nearly my death also. I was born an identical twin. Together we weighed only slightly more than five pounds. This fact alone was serious enough. The birth occurred in a two-room farmhouse, attended only by a local midwife. When it seemed apparent that these emaciated premature infants could not live, a doctor was summoned from the nearest city twenty-five miles away. He had the wisdom to take us in his car to spend several weeks in a hospital incubator. On the following day, the local gossip reported the birth of twins at the Schmitt household with the following note, "One child was born dead, and the other was nearly dead." Since we were identical children and could not be distinguished for months afterwards, I am not sure whether it was I who was reported dead or only nearly dead.

I remember vividly my encounter with death at age seven. The scene was still the primitive Saskatchewan village. My health had slowly deteriorated until one night I went into convulsions. A car was located among the relatives, and then I was taken that long distance over a dirt road to the hospital. Since it was days before I came out of the coma, the kinship again assumed that I could not live. The many months in a strange city, with everyone speaking a foreign tongue, namely English, and the repeated surgery created an atmosphere that death for me was imminent. I can still feel this sensation. Is it the fact that I again outwitted death that urges me to befriend this unwelcome guest?

Life in an isolated prairie village made death always vividly present. The body was prepared by the women-folk, including my mother. The grave was dug by the husky young adult males. The coffin was built by the most skillful local carpenter. There was no escaping death; no neat purchased service could hide the obvious. When death occurred, every one of the one hundred villagers had to get involved if in no other way than to attend the funeral or at least see the men closing the grave with shovels in the graveyard on a hill overlooking the entire village. Most of all, every loss was deeply experienced by everybody since it left a void in the network of relationships. The grieving could not be avoided since all families were represented in the one-room school-house, the one church on Sunday, the local grocery store, or the post office.

I can still recreate the drama of every death that occurred in this village of my childhood. The deaths are even milestones by which I space the twenty years I lived there. I can feel my age and size at the time of each death, and most of all the particular effect it had upon the total community. The one apparent murder was the most overwhelming; the next were the several accidental deaths; then the long, lingering death of several younger people; and finally the more natural departure of the respected elderly.

I wonder if this kind of raw encounter with death, with no protection, did not force me and all our ancestors to dialogue with death and thereby find a different meaning to life.

The most positive effect of this experience is the wholesome communal grieving that I recall. Every detail of each death was told over and over again with every person, to the youngest child, included in the conversation. Those persons closest to the deceased obviously knew the most and thus were most sought after for information. What a lesson on caring for the grieving! What a natural healing process, even for the most acute loss!

As young adults, my twin and I accepted teaching positions in an even more primitive community of "my people" in the far northlands of Saskatchewan. There, life, like the weather, the droves of mosquitoes, and the nightly howl of the timber wolf, was really cruel. The simple piety of the people included a very strong belief in the glories of "life after death." There had to be some place worthy of existing, for the grueling torture of fighting the elements for mere survival made life hardly worth choosing.

Late one night as we were preparing our lessons by the light of a single kerosene lamp, an old man walked into our "teacherage" without knocking. At the doorway he solemnly announced, "I have chosen you boys to build the coffin for my wife. She died this morning." Obviously you didn't ask someone, you bestowed the honor upon the builder of your coffin. We understood immediately and followed him outside to unload the lumber, the lining, and the paint into the rear of the classroom building. On the back side of a calendar page he had sketched the shape of the coffin, including the dimensions. She had apparently been a very large woman. To this he only commented that she worked hard all the years of her life.

The next day the children calmly accepted the presence of the material although it was a sad, somber occasion. We dismissed the students early to begin the construction.

We finished at midnight, including the first coat of paint. The second coat was applied as the children arrived the following morning.

The coffin in the back of the classroom provided the occasion to talk freely about this death and about death in general with the students—my first class on death and dying. The padding, lining, ornamental hinges, and carrying grips were added that night.

The following morning, just as unannounced, the old man arrived with the truck to pick up the coffin. He examined it carefully before he simply said it was acceptable. Then he invited us to the funeral that afternoon and for a light mid-afternoon lunch at his house.

Classes were dismissed at noon since everyone was expected at the funeral. The service was hours in duration, with a eulogy that retold the woman's entire life, emphasizing all the births and deaths that had preceded her. Then there was a final recognition of the "two schoolteacher carpenters who built such a fine coffin."

Death was naturally a part of life in this "bush country." It was not only respected but also welcomed. The funeral service left a distinct feeling that the departed was envied, having successfully passed through the veil of tears. All joined in for an appropriate closure to a toilsome life and then went forth to continue the struggle until it was their turn.

Coming to the United States gave me a second lesson on death. This time it was on how a highly civilized society handles it.

As a young, penniless college and seminary student in this big, fertile country, I took every opportunity to save or earn money so that I could continue my quest and not have to return to bleak and cruel western Canada. A funeral home in the college town offered me a free apartment for answering the telephone, accompanying the ambulance on emergencies, or picking up the bodies of the deceased at night. Any additional time spent in preparing the body, acting as doorman during viewings, or assisting with funerals provided additional pay—a neat ticket to an education.

The socialization process was effectively accomplished. I was very teachable. The efficiency, the cleanliness, the systematic way of picking up, preparing, displaying, and finally disposing of the body without involving a single family member except to pay for it, was far superior to the cruel experiences of my past. I was so overwhelmed that I asked no questions; I only learned my part. To be told on my first day of orientation to pick up free a complete outfit of new clothes at the finest men's store—a Hart, Schaffner, and Marx, no less —certainly helped the education process. There was an exact funeral home posture, facial expression, and word for every occasion that had to be learned. "Oh, I'm so sorry to hear that, Mrs. Jones, but we will be right over."

"Mrs. Jones, we are now ready for you to come here to choose a service. May I pick you up in half an hour? Oh, no! Don't bother, I am ready to come right now. It has been hard enough on you, let me get you."

"Now remember the price you see is for the entire service including opening and closing the grave, and also a concrete

vault. You may want to see this one, too. It is made of solid
bronze. And just to know that this is the final act of gratitude
you can do for your husband."

"Yes, Mrs. Jones, he will be ready for you to view shortly.
May I come get you so that you can be the first to see him? We
want you to be entirely satisfied before the viewing. Oh, yes,
your bouquet has arrived and so have twenty others. Yes!
They are all on display. Your husband must have been a very
well-known man."

"He looks so peaceful. He deserves his rest."

"Oh, you are early, Mrs. Jones, but do come in and be
seated. The people will be coming shortly. The paper said
seven o'clock."

"Mr. Jones, you said. And how did you know him? Oh,
yes . . . just follow me. Mrs. Jones, these folks knew your
husband at the Rod and Gun Club. They want so much to
meet you. Yes, he does look so natural. . . . The flowers
your club sent? Yes, they are right here. That was so thought-
ful of you. And don't forget to sign the register as you leave."

"Oh, Mrs. Smith, I am so sorry to hear that, but we will be
right over."

"Oh, how tragic, Mr. Alexander. We did hear it on the
radio. We will go get her immediately. Thank you for calling."

Then one day, years later, I had to open the subject again.
When I began to dialogue with death, hundreds of people
joined me.

3

a student dialogues with death

Death is always near if we dare to permit ourselves to notice. This becomes blatantly clear when one chooses to teach a course on death and dying. Students frequently voice a fear that there is a correlation between getting involved in the subject and the occurrence of death. This is a very obvious superstition, but a frightening subject like death rouses deep feelings and thoughts.

To teach the subject of death means that one must be ready to handle death and grief in the students' immediate experiences. These experiences make excellent teaching material.

While teaching this course to a group of Catholic seminary students, the father of one of them died unexpectedly. The students were nearby in the dormitory when the news arrived. Immediately they collected all their resources to help their classmate and the entire family through the total experience. All of the class sessions during this time were devoted to processing their experiences and to plan a further course of action. The grieving student used one whole class period to tell the story of his relationship with his father. The biggest loss to him was that his father would not be present at his ordina-

tion, scheduled only a few months later. This experience
became the key to the success of this course, and twenty more
priests have dealt with death differently since that time.

On another occasion when a guest described the struggle
with cancer, a student dissolved in tears. Only the week before
her mother had been diagnosed as having cancer, and she
had a tentative signal that she might also have it.

Then there was the student who had a "death scare" due to
a kidney problem. You are invited to take the journey with
her by way of her journal:

March 20
Here I sit attempting to converse with death, and
I find myself extremely confused. In a sense it's all so
real to me, and yet in another I just cannot comprehend
that I could actually meet death in the not too distant
future. This isn't the first time that I thought about you,
death, but it's the first time that I've put you down on
paper, and this, in a sense, makes you all too real—a
little too real for comfort right now! One minute I think
that I can accept you and the next, forget it! One minute I
realize that I may get to know you a little before I
had ever dreamed I would and the next minute you seem
so very distant—it just depends on how the day has gone.
But I've recently come to realize that even *I* will die
and that you are coming a little closer each day.

Right now I feel anger, fear, resentment, and even
disbelief about and toward you. There is so much that
I want to do yet, and you have almost no right to come
into my life right now. I know that age doesn't make
any difference, but gads, I'm twenty-two, I'm just not
ready to accept you, but then again who ever is? There
is so much in life, and just so very much that I want to do,
I'm just not ready for you to begin to push yourself
into my life. Maybe I will be in time. I've often heard
that as time progresses an individual gets more and more
ready to meet you. I guess that maybe I'm in the state of

denial which all people must go through—but I get
angry at myself for fitting into any of the categories or
models. *I feel* like I should be different from everyone
else, yet *I know* that I'm not, and this almost in a sense
hurts. I want to be realistic about my own illness and
get angry with myself when I see that I'm drifting into a
phase of denial, or disbelief that it's happening. It's funny,
but with my clients I respect their phase of denial and
can deal with them around it, but with myself I become
intolerant and want to yell at myself to wake up and
realize what's happening to me.

March 28
   Yesterday I experienced so many feelings and thoughts
—my mind was going round and round in almost a web of
confusion. Too much so for me to attempt to untangle
what was going on. I started to and wanted to write last
night after our visit from Ken—but I couldn't. When
I attempt to ask myself why, I can only say that I was
both physically and emotionally drained because the
experience for me yesterday was an awakening to the
reality that I now feel perhaps I was denying. It's all still
somewhat confusing to me and I don't think, death, that
it's you that bothers me as much as everything else that
was said. What frightens me more was the reality that I
could very well end up going through a great deal of
what Ken did, and I just cannot seem to accept it.
   It's almost as if there are two of me—one being
objective and somewhat realistic, saying that I know that
I could be in for some trouble; it's possible and not so far
away (like Ken said—he never expected his kidneys to
fail, but they did—well that sort of scares me because I see
myself where he was about three and one-half years ago,
and if it happened to him it *could* very well happen to me,
too). Then there is another part of me, inside, that keeps
saying that it won't happen to me because I'm "different."
But the other part says it could, almost seems as if it
wants to hit me on the head and yell for me to wake up

and realize that I am no "different" and it very well might
happen. I'm trying to make myself believe it, and yet
there's a part of me that just feels sort of numb. I've often
said that I feel almost as if I'm playing some crazy part on
"Marcus Welby" or "Medical Center," and soon good
old Dr. Welby or Gannon will whip out and help me, yet
I know this is not true. Especially after hearing Ken
and being able to relate to many of his experiences—it
scares me, and yet I don't know why I'm scared. I guess
being in a position of uncertainty is always bad. Yet it just
doesn't seem like it's death that I'm afraid of. But maybe
it is and I don't even know it. Actually, death, I really
don't think it's you that I'm afraid of but more so of all the
procedures and everything that Ken went through. Right
now that's almost too much for me to handle. I just
can't see myself going through all that. I know that I
may never have to, maybe I'll never get that bad, but that's
what "haunts" me—he never thought he would, either.
It all seems so unreal and you, death, seem almost better
to me than going through all of that. I really do think
that I'd rather die than go through it all, but wow! That's
a pretty heavy statement for me to say because there is
so much living that I want to do first.

March 30
   It's really funny how fear operates. For me, death,
it sort of comes in waves, usually after something spurs
it on. I spoke with my doctor yesterday, and he told me
that I must come into the hospital as soon as school is over.
I can be objective and mature on one hand and say that
I know that I have to go and that I really need to,
and yet on the other hand I just don't want to go, and
all of the rationalization in the world on my part just
doesn't make the fear dissolve. I've learned one thing
for sure—it's totally impossible to be a social worker and
practice on yourself! I've never been so fearful of the
future, and yet now I almost wish that I could make

today last forever, and yet I get so angry at myself for being afraid. I can't even put my finger on what it is that I'm fearful of. Is it the procedures that I must undergo, fear of what they'll find, or fear of you, death? Maybe it's a mixture of them all—I just honestly cannot tell.

April 4

Today I felt as though I was hit with about a ton of bricks. I'm sort of walking around feeling very detached from everything and everybody—like I'm going through motions but am really very separate from all the other people with whom I'm coming into contact. Why? I guess it's just a reality—or the start of one. I went to an oncologist, and no one has to tell me what the term means. Of course, although I want to ask questions, I'm too frightened. I sat there wanting to talk—but couldn't. Boy, am I ever angry at myself for being so paralyzed —but in a sense I was. I just couldn't bring myself to ask him what he really thought. It's a protective covering, but I keep rationalizing and saying that everything is O.K., but I also know *so well* that you don't go to a top urologist, nor do you have a biopsy if everything is O.K.

April 11

I realize that this will sound like a complete "cop-out," but I have not been able to bring myself to write for a while. I'm sick of you, death, and I'm tired of dying! Damn it, this is outrageous. I don't want to die, and I'm tired of thinking about you. I want to live! I don't think it's avoidance because I've thought more about you lately than ever—but I'm just sick of you. Life has too, too much to offer, and I want to take advantage of it. I have so much to do, and I'm really tired of you having to be a part of it!

April 16

Wow! That talk by Mr. Duncan really hit me. So much

of what he said I could feel. There really was a lot that I
would have liked to put out to the class—but I just
can't. I really do feel different than most of the other
kids—sort of like Mr. Duncan's door. Sometimes I sit and
just look at some of the other people in the course and
I'm almost ashamed to admit it, but I at times actually
resent them! I can understand and rationalize for myself
why, but still I do not like thinking *or* feeling like this.
It's just not being fair to them because many have experienced situations, I'm sure, with just as great an impact
on them as mine is to me.

Yet sometimes I question why I have to be experiencing
this now. It just doesn't seem fair.

April 23

Perhaps it's because of my situation, or maybe I would
have felt this way anyhow, but I'm finding it extremely
hard to address you lately. Is it that you seem so realistic
and such a strong possibility? Death, I don't think that
I'm as afraid of you as I am of getting to you. What's
it going to be like, and I truly wonder when?

Everything, in a sense, seems like a dream, and I still
find it terribly hard to believe what's happening. Today
I went to see my one doctor—an internist—
and we spent a great deal of time just talking. He agrees
with the urologist that I must come in for tests and
said that he could not begin to stress how important it is.
I feel a little more panic-stricken than I used to. One
minute I'm numb, the next I'm completely vulnerable
and so many feelings are spinning in my head that I find
it hard to sort them out. One minute I feel emotionally
strong—able to face anything that I might hear and the
next minute I want to run. Even though *I know* it will
follow me, I sometimes feel that if I go away, maybe
I can leave it all here.

When I look at that last sentence I addressed "it"—I
wonder what I mean? "It" could stand for my "illness,"
or it could mean "death."

April 27

I have been unable to really address you this past
week. Death, I really think that I can accept you, but not
without a pretty hard battle first. It's strange, but until
I'm diagnosed and find out really what's going on I just
cannot truly be sure as to what I am writing. I guess
they're just thoughts—rambling on. But my mind is really
spinning, and a certain type of fear comes over me when
I attempt to really see myself as dying. Maybe because
the possibility of it being true is within grasp right now,
and that is very different from just *thinking* about it.
I'll be going into the hospital May 8th and, in a way,
want to because the hardest part has been the feeling of
uncertainty as to what is happening . . . fear of the
unknown.

Life has taken on an incredible depth and quality these
past few weeks and I really cherish it so much.

April 29

In an attempt to communicate what's going on in my
mind right now—it's a combination of so much. Fear
of entering the hospital and of what they might find, and
yet a certain calm about me that says to just take it all
one step at a time.

When I try to write my obituary, I find three dates
come into mind. One says that it is possible that while
in the hospital something could go wrong. This means
that I would die between May 8 and May 20. Although
I find it hard to believe, it is a possibility.

The second is a very curious date because it just popped
into my mind and so I decided to leave it—April 4, 1977.

The third, and naturally the easiest one for me to deal
with now, would be in about 2030 when I'd be
seventy-eight years old. It would be "safe" to direct my
death to 2030—but at present I just cannot help but think
that realistically the possibility remains that I could die
much sooner. (But, in a sense, everyone *could*. It's also
possible that I'll get hit by a car today, I guess.)

It's not that I can't accept writing an obituary—but right now I just don't know where to direct it. I realize that most people never do—but at present my situation is making it a little too difficult for me to write.

There's really not too much more that I can say right now, except Dr. Schmitt, thank you so much. This class really touched me, and in all honesty, this was one of the most powerful, feeling, sensitive, and beneficial courses that I've *ever* experienced.

Wendy M.

4

teaching death and life

What does teaching a course on death and dying do to one? It is simply a profoundly beautiful encounter between persons who for once bare their deepest fear, namely, the fear of death, with each other. After that, we are free to share many other raw emotions also. The end result is an intensely meaningful experience. It moves from a compassionately human relationship to a spiritually transcendental union.

This letter, enclosed in a death and dying weekly journal, illustrates the point:

Dear Dr. Schmitt,
    I have put this letter—this last entry to my journal—
off as long as possible. It is very hard to end. There
are so many feelings that I have resolved. There is so
much that I feel about this course—how I have lived with
it, how I have experienced myself and others in a new
way, and how I feel bound to you now. I do not know
when or if our paths will cross again. I am somehow
clinging to a relationship I feel with you. I have shared
much in this journal. The momentum has built up,

and I feel like going on and on. However, I know that
tomorrow brings the finiteness of our class into clearer
focus, like the finiteness of existence. I do not want
to end the class or to end with you. The feeling is almost
indescribable. But, I guess it is sufficient to say that you
have touched me and I have grown.

I want to leave something of myself with you. . . .
Since you and I are in a similar process of ending with the
school and each other, perhaps you understand this
letter better than anyone. In this ending I fear the threat of
nothingness. Your leaving the school is a loss of something
rich and valuable, a loss of a feeling-oriented way. I
feel that it is terribly sad. I guess I will have to conduct
my life as a living example of what social work is at
its best.

I feel at one with the universe and all existence. I know
a hymn that I want to share. It speaks of ultimate union.
It speaks of relating to each other without filters that
separate. It describes the union between life and death as
I understand it. I love it.

> Blest be the tie that binds
> Our hearts in Christian love;
> The fellowship of kindred minds
> Is like to that above.
>
> Before our Father's throne,
> We pour our ardent prayers;
> Our fears, our hopes, our aims are one,
> Our comforts and our cares.
>
> We share each other's woes,
> Each other's burdens bear;
> And often for each other flows
> The sympathetic tear.
>
> When we are called to part,
> It gives us inward pain;

> But we shall still be joined in heart,
> And hope to meet again.
>
> *Amen*

My dear, dear Dr. Schmitt, I wish you love, peace,
and happiness.

> Fondly,
> Mrs. ———

My dear Mrs. ———,
It is letters like yours and students like you that
convince me that every human being should stop now and
begin a dialogue with death and then observe the outcome.
As I read of your experience in class and of so many
similar ones, I feel like we all ascended to a mountaintop
in that class—maybe the Mount of Transfiguration—
and there had spiritual communion. From that vantage
point we saw all of life, from birth to death, from eternity
to eternity in a new perspective. It is here that we truly
met and knew the meaning of love. At that moment we
knew the meaning of true human kinship that spanned
all our vast differences of age, of sex, of race, and of
culture. Your selection of a hymn so aptly affirms that we
must part, but not for long. After that it shall be forever.

> A kin in Common Humanity,
> A. Schmitt

Some students take great leaps forward in their personal
growth during a course on death and dying. They return to
unresolved traumatic scenes of the past and permit themselves
to relive them. Now that they know death can be experienced
differently, deep, intense emotions emerge which they can risk
sharing. The healing that occurs is apparent in the following
extended excerpt from a student's journal.

September 25, 1974
There have been so many deaths of those close to me—

sister, brother, parents, in-laws, and a niece. The near-deaths, my son-in-law, John, with cancer; an amputee; and my husband with a bullet still in his head.

I have been there. I have seen death. I have felt the death of loved ones. I have thought about my husband's death.

My husband and I finally signed our wills. We did not arrange our funerals—we only talked about it . . .

He doesn't like to consider that he may outlive me. He says he'll move into one room and draw within himself. Not I . . .

September 26, 1974

I need to talk about death.

I feel compelled to talk about death—not death in the abstract or even the death of someone I've known or heard about.

I want to talk about my own experience with death.

John doesn't like to talk about it. It still hangs over him, and he's afraid. I said I wished he could be part of the seminar.

September 28, 1974 (the morning)

I was too "dead" to write last night.

"You're growing up," was Dr. C.'s way of sugar-coating the fact that I was moving into "middle age." I haven't quite accepted it yet. Just this morning I had renewed evidence that the jig was not yet up and that, even though last week I heard the middle years described as ending at fifty-five. Only months away from that, I am not growing up or even becoming middle aged. I am growing old, and even in my family where longevity is the rule, if cancer doesn't kill you, growing old means eventual death.

Growing up is beautiful! Always the youngest, I had to wait forever to grow up. My brothers still won't recognize it, and I'm not sure I fully believe it myself.

Being grown-up means to be viable, to respect yourself,

to be respected. I've just begun to make it. Really, I'm only just learning how and sometimes, like yesterday, I was so gripped by fatigue. I feel like it's all over. I've lost it before I really had hold of it—through lack of time and strength I've lost it—become ineffective—becoming old, senile, worse than dead . . .

I don't think I really mind dying. My husband assures me he's almost been there twice, says there's nothing to it. You just let yourself slip away. I have no trouble believing that. I've never envisioned it otherwise.

It's not really the dying—it's not even the growing old. It's what goes with old age . . .

It embarrasses salesgirls when they find me suppressing my aging self in the mirror . . .

God help the poor men who will eventually have to fit me with dentures and bifocals. While I imagine I won't take either easily, I've no doubt but I'll eventually take them—same as the next one.

The thing I can't see myself accepting is the loss of my viability.

I am Rachel—committed to striving, to growing. If I yield that to old age, then I will no longer be me—and that is much worse than death.

And yet, even as I write this, I can remember when I thought my life was in bearing and raising babies, and that when I could have no more children my life would be over.

I gave up bearing babies twenty-three years ago. I found there was also more to life. I was glad to see the last of my children raised and gone. I am ready—even eager—for nature to remove the monthly reminder of my fertility.

That part of my life is over, but my life is certainly not. I would certainly not turn back my years for anything—nor would I want to give my life up. I love being where I am. I love it. I'm not trying to hold it static—that would destroy the process—but to savor it and try to develop trust that just as I found these phases

different from earlier ones, and richer, I may find some
of the excitement of growing up even while I'm growing
old.

Isn't it ironic? Here I am celebrating life in preparation
for death.

In the next entry this student, now in her mid-fifties, writes
about a death that occurred almost forty years ago. At that
time, her sister was thirty-two years old and the mother of
several small children. The student was then a teenager.

October 9, 1974

My mourning of her is long since past. It's been years
since I've yearned for a sister in general, or Edith in
particular. But that which I was robbed of—the process
of her dying and our mourning for her—I will be forever
stuck with.

Not that I was the only one who was robbed. Edith
herself was—hence the long coma. Her children were
robbed. I contributed to the theft, "to have her shipped
to the country for her recovery." She was never told
but only guessed, way after the fact. Oh, how she was
robbed! Mother who fainted when reality reached her
consciousness and who, after Edith's death, retreated
to senility, except when Dan needed her.

My brothers with their promises—and their quiet
disappearance.

Bob—her husband—my villain—a victim like the rest!

We were all in it—needing, wanting, yearning to deny
the truth and when we could no longer deny, to forget,
at whatever the price!

I am angry!
I am angry for Edith who died alone—
    no matter who was around her,
        Edith died like an animal.
I am angry for myself who was denied the right to know

The right to process
The right to mourn
The right to live through my own sister's death.
I am angry that I must forever be angry—
forever impoverished.
My mind is divided.
Should I take the plunge—
allow myself to feel it?
Follow my impulse to pour it out—
Share it—
Share it? Lay it on anyone who will listen?
Or should I discipline myself—
hold it back?
Listen a while
encourage the others
hear their fear?
Or am I too busy with my own outpourings?
Or am I afraid I will be consumed?

Edith!
my sister
my mother of sort

Edith!
You left me with a mess
It took time and strength and so
much more to get out of—
What a mess!
Dr. K. asked if I had gotten over your death.

Ruth Ann said the trauma of my life
So untimely a death
for you and yours
for me and mine
We are separate—
Hell! we weren't then
not quite!

Edith, I think we wouldn't have
  any more together now than I have with the others.

Or maybe—if you hadn't died—
  I'd have stayed with you.

I would have had less reason
  to change.
I would not have become—
  the me as I am
So important were you to me—
  If it took your death to do it—
  I'm sorry it had to be that way.
  But whatever the cost
  I'm glad I've grown
  And if the separation had
    to come through your death
  Rather that than that I should
    not have separated.

What a victorious breakthrough for a student! For years
the pain of a death could not be touched and the simmering
fear could not be faced. Then a guided journey back to the
death scene and she returns from the trip a poet.

After a class in which an eighty-four-year-old lady told of
her orderly preparation for death, Rachel made this final
entry in her journal.

November 13, 1974
  Mrs. Rice accepts life and death with zest. I wonder
if I'll ever attain that. I think not with the special
quality she has of serenity without passivity.
  Passivity—nothingness. Being alive for me requires
intensity. I was so close to going under.
  I cannot fade into death while there is yet life. I saw it
in my mother. I see it in my sister. There is a core in
me that I will not yield to. I will live while I am alive! I

used to say if I *had* to be alive I was going to live.

I fight too hard! I grab too greedily. How can I be graciously serene when I know my own enemy?

I am the tiger that I see.

I am the fear that frightens me.

A final hosanna rings through as she writes her eulogy, the final assignment in this class. She read it in class, like a victory song. It was so appropriate and beautifully presented that all of us dissolved into tears.

Eulogy

With a nephew only months younger than she was, they called her Aunt Rachel from the first. They had other names for this baby sister—*chatzha* (the little toy), or monkey. Her nose ran. She wet the bed, and learning was beyond her ken until the teacher sat beside her, looked her in the eye, and called her by name.

Her daddy chose the nicest of the boys and rushed her down the aisle to ensure that his baby would be taken care of in case he died.

The baby had babies of her own. And she would have continued to have babies had she not thrown the table over and blown the lid off the dollhouse, thereby making an awful mess, but also letting in light and air and room to grow.

She and her husband grew together and, in time, so did the children. She wanted another chance to learn. She got it. She used it. She loved it, and life was very, very good. Who, after all, is lucky enough to get two chances?

She died fulfilled, leaving behind her a husband and lover (one and the same), three grown children (all good), and one son-in-law (also good), but no grandchildren. She always wanted grandchildren. She was always greedy.

Several weeks after this course terminated, I received a

letter from Rachel. Her gratitude to me for having been her tour guide to visit the death feelings is overwhelming.

I wish I could find an adequate form in which I could express my notion that you are an artist in that you enabled us to see living and dying in a different perspective.

One of the innumerable rewards for enabling others to dialogue with death—in the name of a graduate seminar on death and dying—is that I, too, am changed. As I help students take this journey to their ultimate finiteness, I, too, come to terms more and more with the limitations of my existence. And death has made us all more alive!

can a dialogue with death give life?

I have just come from a class on death and dying. My whole being is at peace, as if I have been in touch with my soul. "Why is it?" I keep on asking myself. What happens to me when a group of students and faculty members join in a circle and converse on the subject of death? Why should this bring such a feeling of euphoria?

In class today we met a young nurse whom we shall call Kathy. She is only twenty-three years of age and vibrant with life. She is delighted to have been asked to come to class since this is her mission in life. She has no doubt about it. She must tell as many as she can what has happened to her so as to enable others to experience the joy of living like she does.

Only three years ago, Kathy was at death's door. She had total kidney failure and survived only by spending twenty-four hours a week on a kidney dialysis machine. Every moment, if she permitted herself to think about it, she knew that life would not be long for her. People do not survive many years on such a machine. For eight hours, three times a week, she lay plugged into this machine which cleaned her blood as her kidneys used to do. But they were removed, and she would be dead shortly unless a miracle occurred. To keep herself going, she continued her nursing education in the same hospital. Life was miserable at best for her. Whatever free time and energy were left, she had to use carefully. She studied hard and performed her student nursing duties. Then as the time neared for her dialysis the impurities in her blood would gradually sap her energy until she was groggy and faint. Back to the machine. Study—machine—sleep. There was nothing else to life.

She spoke of that "horrible machine" over and over again. Sure it was a lifesaver, but it took on such miserable connotations since it was her lifeline to existence. "Who wants a horrible monster like that to be your only hope to live for another day?" she screamed.

Complacently we take our vital organs for granted. Our kidneys are all functioning normally. We don't even know we have any, except for the little learning we remember from a hygiene class long ago. Suddenly a surge of gratitude flows through us. Thank God, my kidneys are functioning.

But what if they wouldn't? What would I do? What if I depended on a machine for life? Could I take it? Could I go through it like Kathy?

Then a glossy-eyed student interrupted, "Did you ever feel like calling it quits? Did you ever want to tell them to stop it? Was it worthwhile? Did you not rather want to die than to go on like that? Did you ever want to pull the plug, Kathy?"

"You're damn right I did!" came back the fiery answer.

There was a breathless hush in the room. What an awful spot to be put in! What has modern medicine done to us? Why should a human being ever be put in such a spot— where he can choose between life or death? Should there be a single switch that can be thrown by anyone, including the patient herself, that means certain death? Would that then be murder? Is it suicide? When a machine is built only to keep the body alive but leaves all the rest of existence so crippled, can it be called living? Has the miracle of modern medicine been a blessing at all? Or is it becoming more the prison of death instead?

But Kathy is with us today. She is alive. She is talking. She has a message for the living, and she is proclaiming it.

The miracle happened. Her own sister, just a few years older, donated her kidney. It was a perfect match. Her body did not reject it, and she is alive.

A quiet voice from the corner asked, "Kathy! You are so vivacious, so full of life, so dynamic as you speak. You are making so deep an impact on us. Were you this way before?"

"No, I was not!" with equal emphasis. "Actually, the only way I can describe myself is that I think of myself as having lived two lives. I even call them the first and the second Kathy. The first Kathy died during dialysis. She could not make it long in the face of death. A second Kathy had to be born. This is the Kathy that was born in the midst of death. This is the Kathy that fought to live no matter how difficult the journey. This is the Kathy you are meeting today.

"The first Kathy," she said slowly, then sighed, as she stared into space for a long time. Then she continued, "The first Kathy was a frivolous kid. She lived only one minute at a time. She quibbled about cold food in the cafeteria, about the boredom of surgical nursing lectures, about the unfairness of her parents. Her goal in life was to have fun on the weekends—a date and good movie, or a neat dance. Then back to the salt mine. The future was far away and of little concern. Even marriage and a family were of no concern to her. She lived for trivia only.

"But the second Kathy—that's me now. I am infatuated with life. I wake up in the morning and I could scream, 'I'm alive, hallelujah!' Look at the beauty in the sky! It's gorgeously blue! I go into a flower garden, and every flower takes on such fabulous colors that I am dazzled by their beauty."

Then someone in the room remarked, "You sound like you are on a drug trip."

"You're right—I've told myself that over and over again. I'm on one great big high. I'm on a trip, too—the trip of life —and it's gorgeous."

"But, Kathy, is life like this always?"

"I'm so busy now that I have no time to let it be anything else. No sooner had I graduated with my degree in nursing than I was asked to join the faculty of my school. And the main class I now teach to student nurses is death and dying. Besides this I am asked to speak to groups, churches, and nursing classes all over the place. And I *love* it!"

That last sentence was said with a gush of feeling that left no doubt in the room.

"It's just like I now feel. I could put my arms around all of you and hug you to death because I love you so much. I'm delighted to have this beautiful experience with you. You seem so courageous to be in this class—to want to learn about death in order not to be afraid like all the rest of the people around. And you are going to help others not to be so petrified by death that they cannot live. That's just terrific. Then to think that I could be part of this experience with you."

Someone in the room caught the irony of the situation. "Do you know, Kathy, you almost sound like you're advising us to have a scrape with death like you had in order to really live!"

"That almost sounds absurd—but one thing I do know, had I remained my first Kathy, I would have played away my whole life, and I would never have known what the real joy of living was all about. I had to face death eyeball to eyeball before I could live. I had to die in order to live."

The class ended with a standing ovation, and Kathy burst into tears. A number of students and faculty caught her up in their arms as she was kissed over and over again.

After the seminar we gathered into small groups, each led by a faculty member, to process our experience.

"I can't see what happened in that room," one student began in my group. "I thought we were talking about death, and the room was vibrating with life. I haven't been so alive in years. I can't understand it. It's weird."

"You know," another continued, "I'm beginning to think that this class is actually becoming one great big encounter with death. Then when we walk away from it, and know we are alive and healthy, we suddenly realize the whole future is ours to live. We tune in on life like we never have before.

"That is exactly what happened to me last week when we were at that dying professor's house and heard him speak. I ached and hurt as he spoke. He was in such horrible discomfort. His voice was so faint. He struggled for every breath. Each sentence came so slowly, so haltingly. I marveled at his courage. I was torn apart by the whole experience. Then when I left the house I suddenly felt so free, so light. 'I'm alive,' I said. Then the next thought occurred. Now isn't that a dumb thing to say? But life is marvelous—just to be alive. It was drizzling, I remember, but I suddenly saw beauty on what should have been a miserable experience on a dark, cold, rainy Philadelphia street. But I felt just great. 'I'm alive, and that's terrific,' kept coming back to me. I went to my apartment and wrote a letter to my parents. It was so full of gratitude, hearts, and flowers that I'm sure they think I flipped. I even told them about the class on death I just had come from. Imagine that! But I know what happened. I had faced death. But it wasn't my death. Thank God, it wasn't my death that I faced. It was my life I faced, and I chose at that moment to live it to its greatest good."

If dialogue with death can liberate me to live, then why not dare to dialogue with death?

Mrs. Larkins spent several years in and out of therapy with no apparent success. She found no meaning for living. Each failure in treatment made her progressively worse. She felt her only hope was to give birth to a child. There was no known physiological reason why this did not happen. Her husband was kind and empathic, but he felt totally unable to reach her despair or to understand her ever-darkening mood. She needed more and more pills to sleep at night and to rise each new day. That her life was caving in was conspicuous to herself and to all who knew her. No one was able to halt or slow down the process.

Then one day, after another unsuccessful trip to her therapist, she began plans to end her life. She filled two prescriptions which she had saved for the occasion. The suicide note, which I was given later, read as follows:

Dear Tom,
First of all let me tell you that I love you and I am in a very calm, honest state of mind as I write this letter. By the time you read this letter, I will be dead. I'm sorry if I hurt you, but I can't cope with the way my life keeps going and I think it best if I just don't live any more.
I know I can never be well just as a person with a severe cancer can never be well. Oh yes! They may be able to live for years with the help of doctors. They may have some good days, but they are only prolonging the agony of waiting for a peaceful death. What I did was not wrong. I have only done for myself what any compassionate human being does for a sick animal when they know there is no hope for recovery. Please try not to feel guilty for what has happened. You are free to do as you please. I hope you will make a good life for yourself.

Love,
Grace

After this she slowly swallowed all the pills and fell asleep. For no known reason other than a deep compelling urge, Mr. Larkins took the afternoon off and rescued her from a certain death.

As far as Mrs. Larkins is concerned, she committed suicide. She was very aware of what she was doing. Each pill she took made her more certain that the end was near. Her decision felt right. There was no possible return.

Not only did Mrs. Larkins wake up, she awoke to a second life—totally different from the one she had ended in death. This couple heard about me and came for what I would call neither therapy nor marriage counseling. Maybe the best description of what they needed was someone to monitor the drastic change that had occurred and to help them integrate this into a new life and marriage style. I felt much more like a privileged observer than a participant therapist. They did need someone to help them program the change, but the motivation, the drive, and the capacity for building new lives was pulsating through their relationship.

Who is Mrs. Larkins now? The one word her friends have used in *vibrant,* meaning literally tinkling with life and enthusiasm. In touch with herself, her life and her husband, her life is now lived to the fullest and is filling many other lives. There is no pressure in this journey. It appears to be so natural a thing to do, as if she has always been that way. People who did not know her before cannot detect that she has not always been this way—a total discontinuity between the two halves of her life. Within a year after the transition, she became pregnant with the first of several children who were born in quick succession. Even the children bear that special mark of awareness that strangers will note. They appear to exude the thrill of living.

My impression now, eight years later, is that this family has discovered the real meaning of the "gift of life" and are now returning it in gratitude to each other and whomever they meet. Mrs. Larkins finds it hard to recall her former life. It is as if a stage curtain closed long ago to an old play and a new drama is performing.

What is the relationship of life and death? Why are some people yearning for death when, in fact, it is life that they really want but cannot find? Can man really die vicariously with others and then return to a new life? Is the whole atmosphere of denial of death a fear of paying the price really to live?

6

dialogue with suicide

As I stepped across the threshold of the funeral home, I was engulfed in an air of coldness and mystery. She had taken her own life. What else should I expect?

People are baffled by suicide. No one, ever, has the right to take his own life—so says the tradition of the church and Western society.

As I drove the fifty miles to attend this occasion, I had ample time to reflect. I needed to prepare myself for the needs of the people who would silently scream at me. I must be ready.

At one time there was a ritual for handling such deaths, but now there are none. Then, the whole community reacted uniformly with ghastly bitterness. The minister took the occasion to spell out clearly the power of the devil. With no doubts left in anyone's mind, an unfortunate person had willfully walked into his awful snare, and the evidence now lay before all of them to see. Then, for a perpetual reminder, the body was buried outside the boundaries of the graveyard of God's elect. For years afterward, a stigmatized family lived under this cloud whose influence could even permanently bruise the personalities of the descendants.

"What can I now do to bring healing where there is such blatant agony?" I kept asking myself.

"Oh, God! Into your hands I commit myself. Use me—I am ready, no matter how great the need. I love these people. Especially Bob, I love you. I am coming for you. God! I care! Then you are with me!"

The inside of the funeral home reminded me of a cavern —dark, cold, and clammy. Small clusters of people, scattered throughout, were quietly mumbling or silently staring into space. A background of sickening recorded religious organ music created an atmosphere of eeriness all of its own.

In a moment the funeral director descended upon me. His mechanical politeness was almost more than I could take. I was tempted to tell him to "drop dead and leave me alone until I can get my bearings."

When I hesitated to tell him my relationship to "the deceased," he informed me that there was no public viewing, in other words, go away. Obviously the stereotyped mannerisms of his profession didn't quite carry him through this occasion, especially when he had to greet a nonstereotyped visitor.

I then asked for Bob. The funeral director suggested that I wait at the door. Bob rushed over and introduced me to the funeral director. Now his extreme overcordiality, with a repeated insertion of "Doctor," again exposed his feeling of helplessness in a situation like this. He then vanished.

"Oh, you poor creature," I thought. "I guess there is no way you have come to terms with death by choice, even if you are the professional death-dealer in our society, maybe better defined as the professional death-denier."

Bob fell around my neck as he sobbed and uttered over and over again, "Thanks a lot for coming."

He then took me through a heavily draped doorway into a small chapel where Becky's body was in an open casket. "That's not Becky," he said. "It's only what's left."

I added, "Yes, I know." Her face was bloated and bluish,

a sharp contrast to her former lean and pale appearance. He informed me that in cases of carbon monoxide poisoning the capillary system collapses, making embalming almost impossible. The fluid doesn't really penetrate the outer surface which means that much of the blue dead blood remains to discolor the skin.

"Really, she is gone. This helps to affirm that," he said. He remarked that to look at that (he pointed to the body) left no doubt in his mind.

I moved away from the casket as I asked him to come over and be seated with me. I told him I had written a eulogy that I wished to read in the service, and I wanted to read it to him first. I had no sooner begun than he objected. "It's too personal," he said. "It will only upset my in-laws."

I assured him that it might well evoke tears, but what else ought these people be doing at this time? "I can't stand the ghastly silence that is present in those little clusters out in the hallways and the adjoining rooms. What else is there to do but to cry? Besides, someone has to speak for the deep ambivalent emotions and the unanswered questions that are screaming to be expressed. The stoic faces out there mask the inner turmoil."

"Go on, read the rest," he said abruptly.

After I finished, I said rather firmly, "Bob, let me do it!"

"I guess you know best. You were right about having this funeral. I would never have had it if you hadn't insisted. I would never have laid my eyes on her body again after that horrible experience in the garage, but the family needs this. And I know, no matter how painful, this is best for me, too. So go ahead."

I put my arms around him and said, "Thanks, Bob, see what will happen."

I asked Bob to introduce me to all the people who were waiting. They received me with a lot of awareness that I had been involved in Becky's life. The unspoken, haunting questions were legible on their faces. The family concurred that for me to give a eulogy was appropriate.

The pastor arrived only minutes before service time. He looked and behaved overwhelmed. He repeated apologies that he didn't know Becky and Bob, trying to convince me that he was justified in "having only a few words to say."

When I told him that I had a prepared eulogy which I wished to present, he placed his hand on his forehead and breathed, "Thank God." He made a desperate effort to persuade me that it was inappropriate to have a committal service at the end since this body was to be cremated, not interred into the ground; therefore no graveside service could be held. I knew better. It is the soul that needs to be committed to God, and that he couldn't do.

As I walked away, I grieved deeply for this pastor and hoped that a new breed of pastors would soon emerge who would be able to deal with death, not responding to their own fright but rather to the needs of people. No wonder we grieve so poorly—those who ought to help in the healing process are the most wounded. I guess this is another example of Chaucer's famous remark about the rector: "If gold rusts, what will iron do?" Or, "If pastors are petrified with death, how do parishioners feel?"

The coffin was quickly closed. The drapes of the secluded sanctuary opened, and the people moved into the few rows of chairs. The pastor and I were directed to take designated seats up front. Since I faced the approximately two dozen people, I took the occasion to sense their mood. The family in the front row was sullen and stone-faced. The few former classmates and friends behind them were expressionless. All were too shocked to cry.

The pastor took his place at the lectern and quickly went through an abbreviated ritual. A stream of pious words poured out in a learned monotone. He lost his place several

times and shuffled his pages desperately. The eerie atmosphere
became more dense.

I kept telling myself that this horrible scene must be
broken; it couldn't be left this way. Emotions were so intense
you could almost taste them; yet there was not a tear in the
room. "What in heaven's name are these people going to do
with their feelings?" I was about to scream. Is suicide so
horrible that people destroy each other with it, even today? I
knew they used to do it overtly; that at least could be talked
about. But this! Then the dead were damned to hell, and
the living severely reprimanded lest they flirt with the devil. I
imagine that the family could at least wail if for no other
reason than for their sins or for their failure to pray for the
deceased. But now, they were dumbfounded with confusion.
Is this a typical ordeal with suicides?

My processing of the scene ended as I heard my name
called: "The service will end with a few words from Dr.
Schmitt."

The pastor sat down so abruptly that I concluded he was
relieved to have survived the ordeal.

I slowly took my place at the lectern. Silently I opened my
book, then looked over the audience. What ghastly faces! I
turned toward the casket and with deep feeling said, "Becky,"
as if addressing her. I could not go on as her father broke into
audible crying. A number of Kleenex rustled, and I began to
read the eulogy:

"Becky, you were a very elusive and fragile girl! Like the
delicacy of expensive china! We knew about your fragility;
so we tried to hold you carefully. One slip of our fingers and
you fell and broke into tiny fragments.

"You were not made for this world, Becky. It was too cruel
and clumsy for your sensitivity. That faraway, silent look
often told us that you were seeing another world where you
would so much rather be. Your mother was there, and you

wanted to be with her. She left you just when you needed her most—just when you thought you could have her all to yourself. Then she left far too suddenly, and you never had a chance to say good-bye. Oh, yes, you said, 'So long, mom. See you at the end of the semester,' but you didn't mean that to be forever.

"Becky, we understand how terribly painful her leaving was for you. When you first mentioned her death, you sobbed and cried like a little child, and then you begged us never to talk about it again. We kept our word. Only it hurt us even more to know how lonely your grief must have been—that you couldn't even share it. It just simply hurt too much.

"It gives us comfort to hope that your wish has, at last, been granted. You are now with your mother, and we hope you have her undivided attention forever and ever.

"I have confidence that God grants some people the right to choose not to live. I believe he understood that your agony in this life was greater than you could bear and that he will be merciful to you. God knows that man fell into sin and misery. I believe that what you did was more the product of the misery of life—which was no fault of yours—rather than the sin of life that you chose to commit. At that moment you had no free will to choose. The misery of life had been so great for you that you saw no other solution. Death to you was the solution to your life, and you did not mean to create the problem that your going is for us.

"Becky, your husband, Bob, loved you. He told you over and over again. Even in the final office visit when you screamed at him, struck at him, and demanded that he move out of your house and leave you alone forever, he answered, 'I can't, Becky, because I love you.'

"The reason he came back to you over and over again was because he loved you, Becky.

"He loved you far more than most men love their wives, but we also know, for you that was far from enough. You needed to have him totally, every ounce of him—his body, mind, and soul—you needed to help quiet your inner turmoil. Not a fragment of him could you share with anybody. Not even that part of himself that he needed for himself to be a human being could you let him have. But you couldn't understand that no man—no human being—can be totally given away, not even in marriage.

"The reason he left you was because he needed room to breathe and room to grow. He would have shriveled up or suffocated had he stayed. Even you knew this because you told him to leave over and over again so he might live.

"Becky! I find it very hard to say good-bye to you. I cringe to think of your last night alone. How horribly lonely you must have been! This is beyond me to bear.

"When I referred you to a psychiatrist, and when at midnight I had you hospitalized, I knew this hurt you just terribly. Becky, I did that because I cared, but you couldn't understand. You felt only the rejection of being labeled 'mentally ill,' and that was far more than you could take.

"I do remember the many beautiful sessions we had together also. For a number of months you came so gladly and cheerfully. We were so hopeful that the loneliness which had been hounding you since childhood would at last leave you. You were making plans to go to architectural school. Then you lost your apartment and finally your job. To get fired was the last thing you needed at this stage in life. Soon you started crumbling again.

"Becky! We didn't want you to leave. We needed you! You were one of us! You were our child, our wife, our sister, our friend. Your leaving diminishes us because you were a part of us. We are less because you are gone.

"The way you left makes your leaving even harder. It makes saying good-bye so difficult. It's so confusing. We want to blame ourselves, or each other, or you, but we cannot. We are hurting enough without hurting each other more. And I know you wouldn't want us to hurt more, for you knew hurt too well.

"So good-bye, Becky. We hope to meet you again. Forgive us wherein we failed you. We forgive you for your error. Good-bye, Becky!"

During the reading there was a gradual increase in the amount of crying. Every few moments someone sobbed audibly. The father broke into a loud sob when I bid my final good-bye. My own voice broke several times. I let my tears roll without interfering, just simply kept slowly reading on.

After the final adieu, as I looked up through my own blurry eyes, I saw only soggy faces.

As I began leaving the lectern, the pastor quickly rose to his feet and took over. I thought there was to be no committal service, but he was sure of what he wanted to do now. The service was not over. Now, he needed no notes. His voice was clear and distinct. He was looking heavenward as if he were talking to God as he said, "Let us pray!"

"Oh, God, we come to you at this moment when we need you most. We pray for all of us, for we have erred. We failed to extend a hand to Becky when she needed us. When she still was in our midst we hardly knew her. Forgive us, Father! We also pray for churches and their people, for we hardly know how many more like Becky may be among us. People are dying because we don't care. We don't even know them. Move us to care, Father, so that Becky's death will not have been in vain, but that we may wake from our lethargy.

"God, we pray that you will receive Becky and grant her the peace that she hardly knew on earth—and I commit her soul into your care because we know you care far more than we do. Amen."

After the service I believe every person came to me with a single purpose, although in various ways, to say, "Thanks a lot for saying it for me—that's what I also feel."

One young friend handed me a homemade card which had the newspaper obituary glued on, all covered with sticker snowflakes. In pen she had written the simple verse: "Winter comes and goes. As you did."

This was not my last contact with Bob. I especially value the note that arrived a few days later:

On looking back, I feel good knowing that you not only wrote but also read a eulogy at Becky's funeral. Somehow it helped me in dealing with her death, and I feel it helped others also. I'm sure that it also helped you. The eulogy was a beautiful way of saying good-bye for which I will always be grateful.

Thanks again,
Bob

P.S. I'd like a copy of the words.

7

it's an emergency!

"We have a really depressed old woman here at the front desk. You had better get her to one of the psychiatrists in a hurry." These were the anxious words I heard on my intercom. With that began a journey into the grieving process that has not ended even now, six years later. At this time I had given the idea of grief very little thought. I had never read a book on it, nor heard a lecture, nor even seen an article. There just didn't appear to be anything important written about it—at least to my awareness.

"Have her be seated; I'll see what I can do," I responded. I began my usual procedure of handling emergencies that came to the outpatient department of psychiatry at the hospital. This department is part of the psychiatric residency training program of this prestigious school. My particular role was to direct the social service department so that the residents would receive the select training patients they needed. Also it was my task to include the interpersonal as well as the social dimension in the overall training center.

So I picked up my list of residents and surveyed them. Who has taken the last referral? Who has the least cases? Who is assigned to emergency duty for the day? Then I began calling them one after another—all to no avail.

Some said they had received too many new patients recently and couldn't handle another one; others were pursuing special studies and depressed old ladies didn't fit their academic interests. So the excuses continued. The emergency duty resident very abruptly told me that he had enough patients lined up until hours past closing time and couldn't I have her come back the following day when someone else was on emergency duty. The chief resident was not available for consultation. I gave up and went to the front desk to see if I could be of any help.

The receptionist merely pointed her pen to an old lady sitting hunched forward on a chair in the corner of the waiting area, softly sobbing, and said, "Mrs. Alice McFadden —she's yours."

I went over to her and said, "Mrs. Alice McFadden?"

"Yes," she replied as she lifted her tear-stained face. "Are you a doctor?"

I answered, "Yes, a doctor of some kind."

"Can you help me? My family doctor sent me here. I can't stop crying. I'm depressed. He says I need a psychiatrist."

I asked her to come to my office to see if I could be of help—at least tide her over until the next day.

She began talking, but I became intrigued with something very rare about this person. Her clothes appeared of the finest quality but at least a dozen years old and just as out of style. She wore rings and jewelry that were definitely not cheap. Even the handbag appeared expensive, but it, too, was ancient. Her hair was neatly combed into a bun in back. As I trained my eyes on her, I could not believe what I saw. The word *antique* crossed my mind.

As I slowly extended an invitation to her to talk, an unusual story emerged.

She lived alone in center city Philadelphia. Her house was paid for. She had ample income.

When I asked what was bothering her, she managed to say, "I'm so terribly lonely," then returned to her sobbing. I leaned back in my chair. I permitted her to weep, as I tried to collect myself enough to know where to go next.

When I asked why she was alone, she merely shook her head as she cried and mopped up her face with her handkerchief. Even that was of delicate lace.

Slowly she managed to tell me how she had sought help for the past several years from her family doctor. He kept on giving her stronger and stronger medication, but it only lasted a few weeks. Then she was crying again and couldn't stop.

I asked her to tell me more about her present life. She stated that she lived in her large house alone. I wondered why she didn't have someone live with her. All I got was "I can't" and more tears. So back to other questions. No she didn't go visiting because there was no one. No! She didn't ever go shopping. She couldn't. Slowly she revealed more and more of her life that had progressively begun closing in on her. Several months ago the tears began, then sleeplessness, and often whole days in bed, not even wanting to see the daylight. There were frequent visits to the doctor, the useless pills, then finally to this clinic—without an appointment. She simply found her way and presented herself for help. "You need a psychiatrist," they told her. "You are mentally ill."

By now I was aware that all that she told me must have been preceded by a tragedy. So I cautiously asked, "What happened to your husband?" since I already knew she identified herself as Mrs.

The gush of tears was no surprise, but she managed to say, "He died ten years ago."

I commented, "I thought that is what had happened, and I assume he meant extremely much to you." She only affirmed this with a shake of her head.

Obviously she could not talk about the death; so I opened up the subject of their life together. She picked up her head, dried her face, and for the first time talked freely. He was a simply wonderful human being. He was all there was in the world for her. Together they had purchased their house and spent years furnishing and refinishing it. They had made only a few friends, but they were no longer around. I got the distinct impression that the universe for this couple had been only the two of them. Life inside the house became their haven, secluded from the inner-city world. She had never been employed, but he held a prestigious engineering position. He was paid a very good salary with good benefits and a retirement plan.

As I asked questions about this time in their lives, she became free and spontaneous, and the heaviness of the atmosphere lifted. The reminiscing was pleasant; so she kept on wandering to and fro in their marriage. It lasted only twenty years because they were in their mid-thirties when they met and obviously too old to have children. She said they chose not to have them because neither knew much about child care since each had been an only child.

From here she talked in detail about their very fortunate meeting in Philadelphia since neither had any relatives anywhere in the eastern United States.

She became very sober suddenly as she paused and stared into space, then added, "You know, I always had the suspicion that death would come too soon for us and that it likely would be his death rather than mine. I also often thought that should it come it would devastate me—alone in the city, no relatives here, none close anywhere. We had no children. We lived only for each other. We were just so grateful that we had each other. We asked for no more. Then when he was only fifty-seven years of age he had this sudden siege of chest pain. We rushed him to this hospital. He lived only a few days, never gained consciousness."

Now she freely talked about the funeral and the few people that came. She recalled them all by name—mostly people whom he knew professionally.

After this she wept again as she recalled the lonely life since.

Suddenly she looked directly in my eyes and very resolutely said, "I have really enjoyed talking to you. You have been so kind. I have to show you something, but I think you will say I am crazy."

I assured her that in no way would I think such a thought, that what I had seen thus far was just a terribly lonely person who had lost her one and only friend in the world and who had not been able to reconcile the loss. Nothing was crazy about that, nor would anything else she told me change my mind. Her tears were part of a depression and were simply telling both of us that she could not go on living in desolate loneliness any longer. "So please show me, just to prove your trust in me—that I want demonstrated right now."

She began opening up that old handbag. Everything was neat and orderly inside. Just as she was about to open a small side compartment, she again looked up to check my trustworthiness. With this, I extended my cupped hands toward her and said, "You prove your trust, and I'll prove my trustworthiness."

She proceeded to take out a small folded handkerchief and asked once more, "Now you won't think I'm crazy?"

I merely restated it in one word, "Trust."

She opened it up to show me a wedding ring. She added that when she was sitting at her husband's bedside, with him totally unconscious, he suddenly gasped for air, then total stillness. At that moment she removed his wedding ring and folded it into this handkerchief and put it in her purse. For ten years she had carried the purse with her wherever she went, never once looking at the ring, but always making herself believe that her husband was at her side. I gasped, "Oh, that's precious."

"Do you mean it?" came an instant query.

Again I exclaimed, "Absolutely, why not? After all, what the ring symbolizes is unbroken love and faithfulness. So why not celebrate it even if he is gone? You need it so desperately. Who else is there in your life?"

"Oh, that feels so good. Would you say I should keep it in here then?"

"And why not? Do you know, Mrs. McFadden, I feel highly honored to have been the first person that you showed it to—that I should be present when you unveiled it. Would you allow me to hold it too?" With that she picked it up and dropped it into my hands, as if presenting me with a precious gift. I carefully examined the ring to show all the preciousness that this held for her. I then added, "He meant really much to you!"

She again elaborated on her earlier statement and then moved on to the sense of loss that the last ten years had been. Somewhat hesitantly, she next told me that she hoped I would be as kind to her if she told me something more. With a lot of reassurance, she was satisfied. Then she proceeded to tell me that she had not purchased a single item of clothing since her husband's death. What she was now wearing was the best that was left. She also said that there were many items that belonged to her husband that she had never touched, including all of his clothing. Again she wondered how absurd this was. I emphatically stated that knowing how enormous her loss had been I was not in the least surprised. It is even a very common response to so great a loss. I told her about a physician's widow who kept her husband's entire home office totally intact for the remaining fifteen years of her life. She often showed it to people, including me. She, with pride, would point to the stethoscope that had not been touched since he laid it down on that spot. Not until she passed away was the office cleaned out.

She responded, "Why that's even worse than I am, or maybe better!"

I added, "Oh, you!"

She responded with a laugh, "You know exactly what to say!"

I asked her what really had kept her from purchasing new clothes. She stared into space for a while, then said, "Well, I think I don't want to admit to myself that he is gone, and whenever I have been tempted to purchase something, the thought that he would not see me in the new garb was unbearable. For the last several years I couldn't even force myself to go to the store. I only left the house to buy the few groceries that I needed. You know, I have no appetite either any more."

I told her that our time was up, but I was curious about who she was prior to meeting her husband. She seemed pleasant and relaxed as she told me that she was an only child of elderly parents in a small town in Illinois. Her father died, and her mother took up residence in a old people's home when she chose to come to Philadelphia to take a music course. Not long after her marriage, her mother died. Only very distant relatives still lived in that town, but none of them would know her now thirty years later.

With this, she put her ring back into the compartment as I suggested that she return for one more appointment in a week.

Her eyes lit up as she said, "Oh, would you see me again? Oh, you are so kind." She was all smiles as she hastened away.

Deep inside I felt confident that something very important had happened to her during the hour. The thought of her limited life-style and the severe depression haunted me several times. The risk of no medication and of her not having received psychiatric consultation kept coming back. Was I even responsible professionally to trust the session and not get medical backing in my decision? I had never dealt with grief of this magnitude; so how could I be sure I was right? What nerve to assume that one hour would heal ten years of grief! At least she accepted the appointment to return.

One week later, when I was notified that she had arrived, I hastened out to meet her, partially out of relief to know she was back in the psychiatric center.

One sight of her and I knew that we were on the right track. She was dressed from head to foot in a new, very stylish outfit. I responded, "Oh, Mrs. McFadden, you look gorgeous. What happened to you?"

"Well," she said, "that will take some explaining," as we proceeded to my office.

With an air of pleasantness she told me how she had felt as if she had left a burden at my office last week and that she was now free to do what was best for her. That very night she went to a restaurant for a meal, just to celebrate her new feeling. While there, she looked around to see what other people wore, and she felt just horribly drab and inappropriate. She could just tell the way people looked at her. Then she prepared to go shopping, which she did several days later, and planned to wear the outfit to my office today.

I wondered how she gained to courage to do it. To this she responded by saying that she just figured that really her husband always wanted her to dress well for him. So why could she not do it for him now?

From there on the hour was rather pleasant. We even returned for brief moments to her past life, including a stop at the death scene, the coffin, and finally the gravestone. She had visited the cemetery for the first time since the burial on this past Sunday.

We mutually agreed that she had in fact let go of her husband now—not forgotten him, by any means, and why should she? But she let go so that her life alone was not crippled by his being gone.

Then she asked whether I thought she should still see a psychiatrist. I jokingly said, "I wouldn't let you, even if one were available." She said she thought the same, but then she was willing to do what was right.

I asked her how she perceived her future from here on. She said simply, "All right," that she would now just get out of the house. She would purchase more clothes and even find some social clubs to join so as to meet people. She had already looked over the churches in the neighborhood with the hope of finding a church home also.

"Well, then, what does psychiatry have to add to that?" I asked.

"Nothing, I guess," she replied.

I clasped her hands as she bid me adieu with a flood of gratitude.

This experience is what began my journey toward creating a model for participation in the grieving process. The model has served me and many other people very well—so let me describe it.

8

tell me all about it!

The words "Tell me all about it" have become my key for helping others grieve appropriately. This is the exact opposite from the usual statements, "Oh! Don't feel so bad," or, "You'll get over it." Still worse is, "Don't think about it. Think of all the beauty of life still left for you." Or some kindly soul will remark, "It's God's will, so leave it to him."

There are two errors in this kind of advice. First, it is impossible to follow. Feelings cannot be that simply manipulated or programed by one's mind. If one feels bad, especially over the loss of a loved one, a change of mind or getting busy does not get anywhere near the emotions that are hurting. Emotions have to be accepted and handled with tenderness. Deeply hurt feelings heal slowly.

The most harmful element in this kindly advice is that it carries a double message. Behind the words is usually an attempt to stop the grieving person from unloading all the intense emotions that lie behind the grief. These emotions have to do with one's own meaning of life and the fact that it, too, will come to an end, and perhaps unexpectedly or at least sooner than we want it. For most people, these questions have never been faced, not even when they were emotionally able. Now, in the midst of a crisis, they are even less capable of doing it. We have a whole series of kind euphemisms on file to hand to the grieving for the unaware but explicit purpose of telling them to "shut up" because we do not want to be forced into dealing with the issues of death. Yet, to help a grieving person, that is exactly what one must be ready to do.

To say, "Tell me all about it," implies that one is ready to listen to whatever the other wants to say and to hear its meaning for both lives. That is no easy task. It is much simpler to say, "Tomorrow will be better."

Tomorrow will not be better for the grieving person as long as he or she meets people who keep saying this. It will only be better if he or she can be heard. Otherwise, the grief will have to be buried, and on the morrow it will emerge in one of the many usual symptoms: anger, insomnia, helplessness, guilt, purposelessness, and despair. The grieving person could get in touch with these feelings if there were someone to reflect them against.

Tomorrow can be better if we can go on a backward emotional journey with the grieving one. It is yesterday that needs to be dealt with, not tomorrow. If yesterday is laid to rest, then tomorrow will be available to be lived. If the grieving person can be helped to make peace with the past, then he or she will be ready to struggle with the future.

As I say, "Tell me all about it," I envision myself holding out my cupped hands, symbolizing to the overwhelmed person that he or she lay the burden into them and I will hold it awhile. Slowly the grieving person takes it back little by little as he or she is able. The strange phenomenon that occurs is that the admonition to "Bear ye one another's burdens" is in fact accomplished. Fully sharing feelings with a genuinely caring person makes the burden only half as heavy because it is now borne by two people. Mystical or otherwise, to see a person walk away from such a session exclaiming how grateful he or she is, how hopeful the future now appears when it had been so dark, proves that burdens are lighter when shared. Emotional burdens can be shared more easily than financial or material burdens.

I have created a model for counseling that helps me visualize the process of helping the grieving person. The accompanying graphic illustration speaks to me. I use the model in counseling to describe the journey. As we jointly make this venture, I write comments on the chart that are especially applicable to this individual.

If he or she had a beautiful marriage, I add the word *beautiful* after the term *relationship* on the chart. As he or she tells me the date of their marriage, I record it on the line that indicated the first meeting. The years of marriage fit into the space of "life together." I even make it as personal as adding "nightmare due to cancer" in the space "pre-death process." Sometimes I extend the arrow that points to the death toward the top of the chart and quote the comment, "He is now with God."

I have come to call the healing model "Participation in the Bereavement Process." This is exactly what "Grief Therapy," as it is called by one profession, or "Grief Work" by another, is all about. I take the hand of the one overwhelmed with sorrow and walk with him or her through the past relationship and return to the present at the end of each session. This has to be done over and over again until he or she can do it alone without my hand. Then he or she is ready to walk into the future with *hope* instead of *despair*. At this point, my part is finished.

The grieving person is caught in the present. Because he or she has been unable to let go of the past, he or she cannot take hold of the future. On the chart, the lines across the top illustrate the simple facts of the relationship that once was. Two people who once were apart met at a certain point in time

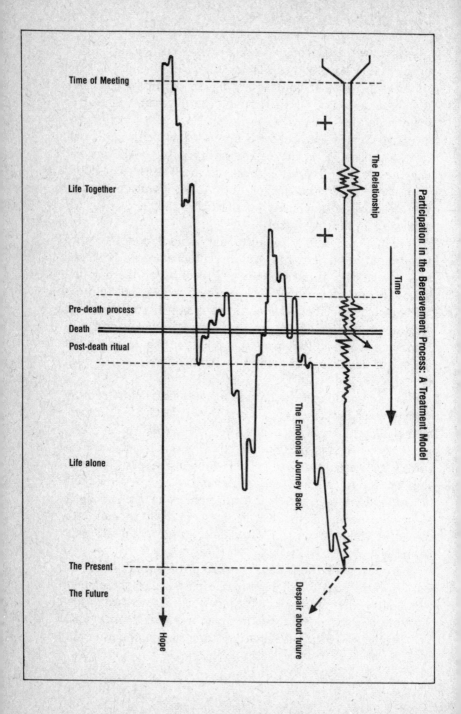

Participation in the Bereavement Process: A Treatment Model

and formed an intimate union. The relationship had its beautiful as well as its stressful moments. The chart shows the good as a straight line and marked with a plus sign and the bad moments with a zigzag line and a negative sign. The purpose of this is to face the simple fact that all relationships have assets and liabilities. This fact clearly shown opens the door for telling the story as it really was, without excessively idealizing the positive and denying the negative. The lines dissecting the relationship point to two very significant moments. One is the time when the fact of the terminal illness was discovered. The second is the exact moment of death. The trauma in their lives is pictured as a "turmoil at sea," as I often call it. After that there is only one line left, and life goes on alone. Often it is very rocky at first, especially the funeral arrangements or whatever "post-death ritual" there may be. It may level off for a period of time largely due to denial or shock. Then when the true impact of life alone hits the person, a new inner turmoil erupts. Some people then scream for help. This is when I see them professionally for "Thanatherapy," as I like to call it, or simply help in healing the hurt of the past.

It is my practice to go over the simple chronological facts of their past as stated above and record the facts on the chart. Then we are ready for the first trip back.

I begin with the present. Where are you now? The most common answer I get is that the griever is nowhere now. Life doesn't count. The past is too painful, the future has no meaning, and thus the present is nothing. Life is not worth living.

My explanation for this feeling of despair which is most commonly defined as depression is rather simple. I believe the person is trying to stop time from passing, so as not to let the distance between the time when the loved one was with him or her and the present get longer and longer. The reason for halting time, I believe, is an unconscious attempt to get back to the scene in the past and finish an emotional task that has not been completed. Simultaneously the grieving one is unable to go back because of the fear of the intense emotions. Since time cannot be stopped, depression is the only psychological method available.

At least then one is not facing the fact of the continuation of time.

I believe the primary task of grieving is to return emotionally to the past so that one can meet the future again with hope instead of despair.

After a brief hearing on the present, I take the first step back. "How has life been since the funeral?"

On this first journey usually the comments are simple and emotionally shallow. "All right, I guess. At first, people remembered me often, but they soon stopped coming. I guess I lamented too much about my predicament. People don't want to hear my sad story. They have troubles of their own." And so on and on.

Then back to the funeral. The people who came, what did they mean to her and her husband? A real crescendo of emotions erupts now as we attempt to stand by the coffin and see him in it. Then the final farewell and grave scene.

An even more intense moment is the exact death scene. This too must be relived. Some people are not able to stop at this on the first journey. They quickly pass over it and into the life together. I only take note of this and go with them where they need to go.

The atmosphere in the office lifts as we venture into the past relationship—detail by detail. At first all the good is sorted out, but I am already listening for the other side. It may only be alluded to briefly, and this becomes my cue to pick up the negative.

When I sense that the person has reached her capacity for the hour, I begin the return journey, picking up a few more new items until we are back to the present. Then I make the next appointment. Often they ask, "What shall I do this week?" My most common answer is, "Be careful with your-self. You have many hurt feelings. Try not to hurt them more. Bring them back here, where they belong. Call me if it gets too painful. Otherwise, I shall see you next week."

The next week we journey back again. It may not be as I describe.

To illustrate this point, I have just seen a middle-aged lady who lost her daughter six years ago in an accident. Although she is the mother of a large family, she has been unable to let go of this one child.

For her second session she brought in a large collection of mementos that she kept in a bedroom drawer. Frequently she fingered through them with only a feeling of pain. These items became the agenda. There was a photo album of every picture taken of this child, neatly arranged in chronological order, with dates and locations written in. After the final picture, she showed me the little cap the daughter wore at the time of the accident. This brought us to "zero hour" in the agony, long ago as well as in the present relationship—the exact moment of her death. Now she had to describe every precise detail. Then the agonizing question, "What did I do wrong so it could have been avoided?" She could finally lay it to rest by concluding that no human being could possibly put in enough precautions in the life of one's family to avoid an accident. To try would destroy the freedom of living and thus make life even worse than death. Then she let go. This was the first time that she permitted herself to cry uncontrol-lably. She remarked, "I could never do it at home for fear of the effect it would have on the other children, but here it is safe."

This entire process can be viewed like the swinging of a pendulum. Emotionally, one needs to swing from the present into the past, then through the present to the future again. During healthy grieving, the pendulum swings smoothly. For some people, the pendulum has stopped and they can live in neither direction. My task to facilitate grief is to begin the swing again—at first short swings, both toward the past and toward the future; then longer swings, until a full, even swing is achieved. The clock of time is ticking again. Life is lived naturally, taking in where one has been in life and where one is going, and living both to the full in the present. With each venture into the past the experience becomes less painful and more consoling. After each return, living in the present becomes more meaningful and the future more hopeful.

I like to think that grief is healthy when a few goals have been achieved. One of these is a need to return to the past, even to the point prior to having met one's departed loved one. I believe this puts the relationship into the perspective of the whole. To be aware that there once was a time, even as there now is, when life was lived as it must now again be lived without the partner appears fulfilling to me.

To return to the death scene emotionally without undue discomfort is another goal of grieving.

I believe to freely entertain "flashbacks" is essential too. The sight of a familiar scene, an item of clothing, or the "chair where he once sat," or even the recall of his favorite joke will bring an instant replay of the past. I believe a goal should be the ability to let this happen periodically and even to deliberately make it occur. When it does, pursue the feeling, the scenery, the episode, and play with it as long as need be. Then peacefully fold it away until it happens again.

The discovery of this grieving model has been of great personal and professional value. For me, the journey back has not only brought acceptance of many losses, including the loss of youth, but it also has helped me yield to my finiteness. For the many grieving people this model has provided a comfortable tool.

Shakespeare said, "Give sorrow words—the grief that does not speak knits up the o'wrought heart and bids it break."

dying in order to live

"I have been asked to talk about my Christian belief on death and life after death. It is a profound privilege as well as an overwhelming task.

"Let me preface my remarks with another statement. I am envious of you students in this course. I would have been so much better off had I taken this course during my seminary days, but there was none."

So began the remarks of a mild-mannered, aged Catholic priest—the guest speaker for our interdisciplinary seminar on death and dying. His voice was soft, at times almost inaudible. He was, without doubt, a man of wisdom who had lived deeply; and he was brilliant, holding a doctorate from a famous European university. At one time, he was a parish priest and a seminary professor; now, a devout human being.

The students wanted him to come and talk about a Christian theology of death and life after death. For that matter, they wanted somebody from every religious faith known to anyone to come—Jewish, Catholic, Protestant, Buddhist, Shintoism, you name it. Anyone who had any light to bring on death was welcome. How do people handle death? Does a faith in life after death help? If so, how? "Come tell us about it. We have opened up ourselves to *death*. Now let us know."

"Courageous kids," I kept on saying. The religious community was nowhere near to dialoguing with death like these students were. My efforts to get guest speakers for these lectures thoroughly convinced me of that. I would follow through every lead I could get for a competent person. All of greater Philadelphia was eligible territory. Most of these calls resulted in no responders.

Our guest speaker made it clear that he was not selling a religious view but that he was going to share the journey with death honestly. He first called our attention to the fact that he was not a young man any more—past retirement age—but he was fortunate to be of sound mind and thus had no reason to stop teaching. "Obviously I have given much thought to my own death. After all, looking at all of you, the chance that I will be the first to die of the people present in this room is highly probable.

"Let me begin by saying that I believe in life after death, that I, as a person, will live again. I know the Bible talks about a future life in words like a new heaven and a new earth— even a new Jerusalem, where the streets will be paved with gold, and an immense wall built around it made of every precious stone known to people two thousand years ago. There is a river of life flowing through that city, and everyone who will drink of that water shall never thirst again. And when God shall wipe away every tear, there will be no occasion to weep again. This is beautiful language. It is a desperate attempt of a mind of that era to describe to an essentially illiterate audience that after this life will come another life that will bring all of their highest hopes to fullfillment. This I believe too, but many of these descriptive terms are symbolic. Many people today do not get beyond the symbols. And that is all right too!

"But for me, I see the future life as being one of continuous

growth, evolution, and fulfillment. When I have a profound
experience in living today, I immediately conceptualize that
this is given me, but as a taste of what I will discover to its
completion some day. Like at this moment I feel present in
this room, comradeship—maybe communion with people. I
feel a search for truth. Then I say, in the life beyond I will
experience this to a far greater degree; and what is more, it
will be an ever-evolving process. I can simply say that to
experience joy, laughter, peace, for moments only, convinces
me that I must someday experience it completely. To me, they
are foretastes of what is yet to come; otherwise they have no
meaning.

"I need now to elaborate, so that you do not think that my
belief of life after death is simply a 'pie in the sky by and by'
religion. It is far from that. Actually I believe in the life after
death because I am already living, to a degree, my postdeath
life. I am now living spiritually my resurrected life.

"You see, my faith is built on complete trust in the historic
Jesus Christ who died and arose from the grave almost twenty
centuries ago. The day that I understood and accepted that
death as being for me, I died spiritually to an old life; and I,
like Jesus, was resurrected to a new life. So I now say that I
live 'in Christ' as the New Testament repeatedly calls it. The
moment I experienced this, my mind ascended to a new level
of awareness of my existence, including peace with my limited
daily existence and my certainty of a future life.

"You folks know about the new consciousness-raising experiences. Well, that is not new. People throughout the ages
have known it as they, like me, were transformed. Christianity
even uses the term *new birth* in an attempt to describe how
totally new the person really is.

"As for me, you see what that means in relation to death.
A very significant part of me has already died and is already
resurrected. And I already live that life; so when my bodily
death comes, it will only be a part that yet needs to die."

At this moment a student interrupted. "Gee! I grew up in Christianity, and I never heard this before. Are you sure this is Christianity or is it Catholicism?"

"This is not sectarian theology!" he quickly replied. "This is basic Christianity. It is repeatedly stated in the New Testament that we who believe in Jesus, died with him in his death. We were even buried with him and then finally raised with him to a new resurrected life now. If any of you have doubts, read Romans 6—it's said as simply as this."

Another student responded, "You describe it so logically, even beautifully. It very obviously has a lot of meaning to you, and that is just wonderful. But why is so little said about this? I am a Protestant. I attend church, but I never heard this description before. Why is that?"

"Unfortunately," our guest replied, "Christian theology is taught by many people. Some are poorly informed. But then you must remember that the idea of 'living the resurrected life now' is no easy concept to comprehend. Most people think only concretely. They need the 'city streets paved with gold' eschatology. Whereas, for many of us, this is far from enough. This idea is an abstract idea, but it is central to all of educated Christendom throughout the ages. We must be tolerant of those who need simplistic and tangible explanations. Unfortunately, many of these people have become the voice of Christianity. The whole movement has been undersold.

"As for me, I am already an heir to my future inheritance. The vicarious death and resurrection is real to me. It doesn't mean that I don't live a human life also. In one sense, I have to die daily to an old life and be resurrected to a new victorious life in Christ."

Again he was interrupted. "Your ideas sound great, but does this then mean you do not now fear death like the rest of us?"

"No, it doesn't mean that. I am afraid also. The statement that comes to my mind is, 'It is not death that I fear, it is dying,' and I do fear dying.

"Now I must come off my priestly pedestal and share something with you that will really add to my comfort with this theology, as well as tell you why I am so glad to be here. I very nearly died on two separate occasions. During the past ten years, I have had surgery twice. Each time I was clearly told that my chances of surviving were poor. In no way did I take that calmly. I only wish I had known about the emotional phases of dying described by Elizabeth Kübler-Ross.* Now that I know it, I went through all of them. I even bargained with God to let me live, and then I would serve even more obediently.

"At this moment I have reason to believe that the same ailment is returning, and I will need surgery again. The thought that it would have been better had I not made it during the last surgery is even appealing to me at unguarded moments."

There was a deathly stillness—if I may use that term—in the room as we stopped this part of the class and filed out to form small processing groups. In the solemnity of the moments, students shared deeply.

"Oh, if I could only believe like he does. It would solve so many problems for me. In my journal I can't let go of the subject of life after death. Somehow I can talk all I want to about dying with dignity, the morality of 'passive versus active euthanasia.' But then I bump into the thorny question, 'What's after that?' Then I halt. Often I dissolve into tears. You see, I grew up in the Catholic church. I attended Catholic elementary and secondary school. I heard all this teaching. Although I must admit I never understood it like today. Then when I went to college, I junked all Catholicism. Taking this course causes all of this to come back to haunt me. But then I knew it would happen. I still went ahead."

---

*Elizabeth Kübler-Ross, in her book *On Death and Dying* (New York: Macmillan, 1970), enumerates five progressive stages in the individual's emotional response: denial and isolation, anger, bargaining, depression, and acceptance.

Someone else stepped in, "Don't you think that you took this course for that exact reason? Maybe you need to go back and pick up the pieces you left behind. I feel such a longing in your voice as you share such intimate information."

She wiped away tears and blew her nose as she responded, "I'm telling you, this whole course has brought back a lot of memories. This is what I took like nearly every time I write in my journal—soaking wet!

"One thing I do know is that I have a lot of homework to do when it comes to dealing with my feelings about death. That priest's lectures certainly hit me hard. Go on with someone else, please. I've had it for today!"

She then said that she had always heard that her family believed in nothing beyond the grave—that only what one accomplishes that has lasting worth in this life will live after one, and that there is no conscious existence after death. "It has always felt good for me to think that way. This is the first time I ever met anyone who was sure of his personal existence after death."

"What a beautiful person!" another student chimed in. "My, if I could reach his age, with my life as well put together as his is. And also to have the certainty of a second life would help so much."

Then another student picked up the dialogue. "What troubles me about him is that I am not sure whether it was his religious faith and the neat way he had it all worked out for himself, or whether his two encounters with death made him the person he is. You know, he reminds me a lot of that student nurse with the kidney transplant. Now she had no religious belief system, and we were all so impressed with the quality of life she had captured."

The session concluded with this student's remarks, "I don't know where you all come out today. But as for me, I go it all the way with that priest. I come from a Christian upbringing. I married a Christian girl whose father is a pastor.

We started out our marriage essentially committed to the same beliefs. Then we got on this intellectual trip and graduate education. Soon we had no room for Christianity and the faith that seemed only for children and old maids. But I now see that when it's all said and done, the answer doesn't lie where we have been searching. I believe in life after death, and I am going to find that life now, even as the Father has. I never knew I would make such a commitment as part of graduate school education. So here it is!"

10

overwhelmed by death—
a real-life experience

"You may use it all because the class was a real-life experience." This was Sheila Scott's instantaneous response when I called her to get permission to use her journal in this publication.

"But you were so overwhelmed by the subject of death, and you say the class was a real-life experience?" was my startled response.

"Yes, I mean that, and you may use it as long as you disguise my identity."

"Very, very good, Sheila, and I will send you an autographed copy of the book."

This chapter will be entirely devoted to the journal kept by Miss Scott while enrolled in my graduate seminar on death and dying. It is verbatim except where I need to describe material that cannot be reproduced. Many journal entries are omitted for brevity, but I believe the essence of her experience is not affected.

My reason for selecting this journal over a hundred others is that it is "real life," dramatically and courageously lived and recorded. It shows the detailed process of a student who dares to dialogue with death in spite of her acute fear.

Well, I've had this book since we were first asked to
keep a journal concerning death and dying. Yet I have been
unable to open the book. . . . That's funny, you know,
I was really eager to take this seminar. I had signed up
for it in September and was disappointed when Dr.
Schmitt canceled the course. This December when we
signed up for the courses I was the second person to sign
up. . . . Now, all of a sudden, I'm afraid and tense. However, at the same time, there's something about thinking
about D and D which raises my curiosity and courage,
hoping I can inwardly confront and deal with my fears
of D and D.

In writing, a particular thought comes to mind. When
I was eighteen, my paternal grandmother died after a
long illness. At her funeral where family and friends
gathered, "sad" music chimed through the funeral parlor.
People openly cried, some fainted, and voices could be
heard saying, "It's such a shame, she was a good woman."
I sat motionless next to my mother in the eighth row
from the dead body as my father sat weeping on the first
row. Everyone in the church then went to the casket
to view the lifeless body except me. Even my ten-year-old
cousin bravely walked to the casket and kissed grandmother
for the last time. However, I could not budge from my
seat, and my mother sympathetically told me it was all
right. Father, from his first-row seat, looked at me with
almost begging eyes that seemed to say, "For *me,*
please go up to the casket." Yet I was too afraid to be
near the dead body. I even visioned grandmother opening
her eyes just as I got to the casket, scaring the hell out
of me. As we left the church, I felt extremely guilty
for my failure to confront death, and later I was unable
to openly face father, whom I felt I had let down. This
incident never left my mind. Often when I'm ready
to go to sleep I visualize the casket as I had seen it from
my eighth-row seat. Since then several relatives have died,
and I have been unable to attend their funerals because
of my fear of facing death. Luckily both parents seemed
to understand my fears and decided not to force me to

attend. However, this only produced a greater guilt
inside me. I feel I have reached the point where I want
to confront my fears. I realized the importance of this
when working with a client whose daughter had been
murdered and the body found in a trash can. I was unable
to allow this client to have a real meaningful experience
with me concerning her feelings about the loss of her
daughter due to my own personal fears. It is time I deal
with the subject and stop running from it.

If one views death as frightening, it is difficult to help
a client face death.

Important to consider death not only for others but for
oneself. Oh, but it's so painful to do!

To think of death is scary because it represents the
unknown.

I called a family friend who owns a funeral parlor.
I asked him if I could visit his parlor as, I explained, I
was taking a course on D and D. I asked him if I could
first tour the parlor and later talk with him. I was
curious concerning his views of death and apparent lack
of fear of dead bodies.

As I was ready to leave the house, I realized I could
not go alone. I telephoned my boyfriend asking him to
go, but he refused, stating he didn't have the time.
Because of my persistence and pressure, he finally agreed
to take me to the parlor and later pick me up. I agreed,
hoping to later pressure him to come in with me.

The trip down to the funeral parlor is one I'll never
forget. As we rode in the car, it seemed as if my heart was
going to jump out of my chest. I also experienced difficulty
in breathing. The palms of my hands were soft and
sweaty. To conceal my nervousness, I began to make
false and phony conversation with my boyfriend and to
smoke heavily. As we arrived at the funeral parlor, I
wanted to say so badly, "Keep on going," but I didn't.
Because I must have appeared so desperate and frightened,
my boyfriend agreed to walk me to the door. As I got
out of the car, I suddenly felt dizzy, and as I walked up

the steps to the entrance, I felt light-headed. Then it happened—I must have fainted. It's funny, I don't remember fainting or falling to the ground. I do remember, as I came to, my boyfriend standing over me and asking frightenedly if I were OK. He then suggested I go back home. I never argued with him as he helped me back into the car. As he never mentioned going in to tell the director what happened, I never suggested it. I realized that deep down inside I wanted to go home! Damn it all! . . .

Today I honestly forgot I had a 9:00 class on D and D. For some reason I felt I did not have to be at school until 11:00 as last semester. However, at 9:00 this morning I suddenly awoke from my sleep remembering I had a class. It was too late, however, for me to make the class. Looking back now, I remember feeling relieved that I had forgotten, and that makes me feel guilty. I knew we were to see a film of a person dying which I dreaded to see since Dr. Schmitt announced it in class. At that time I felt relieved I would not be able to see it. On the other hand, however, I felt guilty as I thought of the other classmates who gathered the courage to go to class. I felt silly and weak, and I still do. I feel bad that they might think I purposely missed class, then rationalizing it by saying I forgot.

As I explained this to Dr. Schmitt, he helped me to look at several things. I now know I am ashamed of my fear of death. Also I have looked at this course as the answer to finally confront this fear, and in several weeks I would be "cured" and able to accept death and the dying process. I also feel I am too eager to be at a stage of acceptance of D and D which I am not ready for. Possibly because I feel many of my fears are unexplainable I hoped to cast them aside and be fully recovered.

This course will not "solve" my fears in seven weeks. At best, it will help me to only begin to confront death for myself and others.

One of the first things I must do is to accept, for whatever reason, that I possess a fear of death, and in my own way and in my own time I can confront the topic if I choose. However, this has to come at my own pace, which should not be judged by the pace of another.

In going to the funeral parlor, I now feel I wasn't ready for that step. I realize I fainted because I wasn't ready at that time. I could not yet make that step to deal with my feeling concerning D and D. I really didn't want to go but wanted to prove to myself I could step into a funeral parlor as others do.

I only hope one day I will conquer a lot of my fears, but until then I must not push myself too fast. Right now I'm fearful of a funeral parlor, and I know I cannot visit one. I can only say I hope in the future I will be able to reach this point, at my *own time* and *pace*. I cannot judge myself by others—mother, father, etc. *"I am me* and *no one else!"*

February 4, DAMN LUCKY TO BE ALIVE *(After this caption which she clipped from a newspaper, she proceeds with a journal entry.)*

I clearly remember January 3 of last year when I was hospitalized to have a major operation, scheduled for the next day at 8 A.M. The day before I was admitted into the hospital, my mother and father took me out to dinner. It seemed as if we all realized how serious the operation was although we didn't talk about it. I remember pretending to be happy and unconcerned about the operation. Mother and father both stated several times the operation was nothing to worry about although it was apparent they were not completely convinced of this.

The day I was admitted into the hospital mother took off work to accompany me. On the way to the hospital, mother stopped to buy several "goodies" which she thought I might enjoy. It was almost like a prisoner about to be executed but first granted several wishes. Mother stayed with me all day, and father came to the hospital after work. As the time came for them to leave, mother's eyes filled with tears as father's looked sullen. I fought to hold back tears. We all seemed to realize I could possibly die as a result of the operation. I remember thinking, "How can I die? I'm only twenty-two years old. I haven't even had a chance to live."

As my parents arrived home, they immediately telephoned to recite a prayer to give us all strength and ask God for strength. That night I didn't sleep a wink but talked to my mother most of the night on the telephone. The next morning as the orderly wheeled me to the operating room, I asked God not to let me die. As I awakened from the operation, my first thought was, "I'm alive."

Until this point I took life for granted. I realized most of my fear concerning death was related to the feeling of not yet having lived life. Those who have lived life are more equipped to face death.

On another date she wrote a meditation on the wrongness of the death penalty. To set the stage for this, she enclosed a picture of an electric chair plus a clipping of a House-Senate conference committee having reached an agreement to bring back the death penalty. Her intense emotions follow.

I strongly oppose the death penalty for any person. . . . The death penalty to me represents a form of brutal revenge. . . . To take the life of another person by way of the death penalty is murder within itself. . . . With our society set up the way it is, minorities would suffer the most from such a ruling. This is one good way to continue the practice of racism.

Next to the picture she added a large scroll saying, "This is so frightening because it has the power to *kill*."

In a later entry she included a course description from another D and D class taught elsewhere. In it she underlined several statements. One rather interesting one was, "An important part of this course will be a field project, such as a visit to a funeral home, in which each student will have to investigate some aspect of death." No doubt this is a reference to her own disastrous attempt to do this assignment on her own.

She also calls attention to several additional statements.

"In this course we hope the students will learn to consider facing their own eventual death more easily and accept better the deaths of others. Hopefully by confronting death themselves and deaths of others, they'll be able to relate this to life and living."

Then she begins her journal again.

The one thing this course has done for me thus far is that I have begun to think of death in not so frightening a way. This is not to say all of my fear is gone because it isn't. I'm afraid of death because I don't know what happens when I die. Is there really a heaven or hell? Does your spirit live on? Will you see others who have already died? Are you still aware of what's happening in the world? Is there a God? Does he punish you for your sins? Is there such a thing as reincarnation? These are questions I have had but before I blocked thinking about them. I presently have begun to think about these questions in greater depth. I don't have the answers and may never have, but at least I think about them.

Although I do not have a preoccupation with death, I do think a lot about the fact I will die. It is true, I have been fearful of living in the fullest sense. I have not trusted my own strength and capabilities but depended upon those of my father and mother. That is why it's so important I experience life on my own. I feel I have reached the point where I must venture on my own.

For many pages Miss Scott is struggling with all her feelings in relation to her uncle who is serving a life sentence for a crime. He had already served five years of the term when she was born. He was only eighteen when he was involved in a series of crimes with a gang of four other fellows. Now, twenty-eight years later, he is being shuffled between a state prison and a state hospital and denied all parole for "psychiatric reasons."

My final exclamation after reading this section is: "No wonder she is overwhelmed by death. It has been an unpleasant guest of this household all the days of her life." But now she is working for a new resolution. Back to her journal:

My only contact with Bill has been by mail and prison visits. . . . For the first time six months ago, I could touch him. . . .

I personally have been impressed with Bill's determination to acquire freedom and his will to live. What is life in his case? For Bill, life is precious and meaningful. It is hard for me to believe Bill still has ambitions, desires to fight back and live. I can only imagine myself crumbling and dying a slow death. I admire him for his courage.

Here is one of the thousands of letters I have written on Bill's behalf:

To the Members of the State Parole Board:

Bill, upon his own confession at 18 years of age, committed a serious crime, but now, twenty-eight years later, he is a completely different person. He is intelligent, articulate, and wants very much to be released. How can one measure the level of desperation or the sense of abandonment a man must feel after so many years?

To say Bill is out of touch with reality to some degree or other may be true, but what reality has he known for more than half his life? The four walls of a prison cell! His long incarceration does not seem to have deprived him of the realities and adjustments that

are taken for granted by those who consider themselves
to be rational beings. . . .

February 13

Well, it's the day before our class visits the cancer
hospital. I'm really "uptight" and nervous about this
visit. I don't wish to see people obviously suffering and in
pain. Suppose I faint again. I'm not going to think about
it again until tomorrow. If others in the class can do
it, so can I. Then again, I shouldn't judge myself by others
in class.

February 14

I was really surprised the visit was not as depressing as
I expected. I really expected to sit in terror.

* * *

What is the meaning of life for me? Life for me
does not only mean achievements, accomplishments, status,
financial success. This is one of the basic problems I
have been struggling with. Life goes much deeper than
that. It is peace and harmony with myself. Life is
experiencing oneself to its fullest capacity. Life is measured
in terms of quality, not quantity. The funny thing is that
I am afraid to truly experience myself. I guess I'm afraid
of pain, or I have a lack of confidence in myself. This
is why it is so important that I leave my parents and strike
out on my own to discover myself and experience my
own sense of self-worth as I attempt to live life to its
fullest with whatever time I have left on earth. In the
past I have measured life in terms of quantity, not quality;
and it's not that way at all.

February 17 (*With this entry in the journal Sheila Scott
has pasted a newspaper picture. It shows a young girl with a
pleading look on her face holding a sign that reads—
"There won't be any children of tomorrow if abortion
kills them all today." This is followed by an entry.*)

I had an abortion a number of years ago. It's
something I find difficult to even think about. I have felt
extremely guilty ever since. At the time, I did what I
thought best. I wanted to finish college and not marry
or have a baby. I also did not want to embarrass my
parents. If I had to do it over, I wouldn't do it. It's a fact
I will have to live with for the rest of my life. I committed
murder!

Then on the following page she inserted an editorial from
an unnamed newspaper entitled "Abortion Issue Revived,"
and she has underlined the statement: "If the taking of the
life of a fetus licentiously—indeed, unwincingly—is wrong,
then it is wrong irrespective of whether the mother thinks it
is right."

As part of the same page of newspaper a Bible text appeared, which it seemed to me she deliberately did not snip
off. I wonder if she is saying this for herself. It is too appropriate to be accidental.

"For the Lord God will help me; therefore shall I not be
confounded: therefore have I set my face like a flint, and I
know that I shall not be ashamed. He is near that justifieth
me; who will contend with me? Let us stand together: who is
mine adversary? let him come near me" (Isa. 50:7–8).

Yes, Sheila, you shall be justified!
The next entry is an exclamation in large letters.

I SAW A PREGNANT ADDICT'S BABY EXPERIENCING WITH-
DRAWAL SYMPTOMS TODAY. IT REALLY BLEW MY MIND.

February 22
We had to rush my grandmother to the hospital today.
She is in critical condition after a heart attack. My
grandfather was extremely upset. It was the first time I have
seen him cry. I was upset too, as was everybody, really.

She looked so pale, weak, and helpless. I wonder if she
is ready to die at age seventy-seven? What can I do now
to prepare myself for the fact she may die? How can
I deal with my feelings yet help my mother deal with her
feelings? It might be helpful to talk about it if my mother
wants to. I really don't know, however, if I want to discuss
it myself. I keep telling myself there is a possibility she
might die, yet I don't want to accept it.

February 24

Grandmother's condition has not changed and the
doctors feel she has a 60-40 chance for recovery. . . .
Grandfather came over for dinner today, and we had a
large family meal: turkey—the whole works. We did not
discuss grandmother at all except to jokingly say she's
finally getting the bed rest she has needed for so long.
Grandfather also joked, it was a good thing grandmother's
heart was in good condition or else she might not be
alive today.

After dinner we went to see grandmom.

She sure looked better.

February 25 *(two days prior to the final class)*

It has been difficult for me to write in this journal. I
have many thoughts in my head but find it difficult to
put them together on paper. Many things have happened
to me since the beginning of this course. These things
have forced me to think what this course is about. I often
wanted to verbally put out my feelings in class, but I find it
difficult to articulate them.

My placement at the drug unit and grandmom's illness
have helped me to consider for myself the meaning of
death for me. But in doing so I had to consider what
life is. I came up with no clear-cut answers although I no
longer judge life by quantity but by quality. Life for me
is to be at peace with myself, no matter what I do. Life is
enjoying every second, living every second to the fullest;

taking nothing for granted. Life is experiencing oneself to the fullest.

On the following page she had another clipping, an excerpt from someone else's will which makes a request for both passive and active euthanasia if the need should arise. It said, in part:

I ask that medication be mercifully administered to me for terminal suffering even if it hastens the moment of death.
If I were dying in pain and misery and being kept alive by some machine or device beyond the moment that I would want to live, I would certainly hope that someone would pull the plug.

Then another burst of fear from Sheila: "If grandmother asked me to help her die, I could not do it. I hope no one makes a request like this of me."

February 26 *(the day before the final class)*
Dr. Schmitt, my grandmother died today. I can't talk about it. Please forgive me. I can't seem to even function.
I had planned to write my obituary tonight. I can't.
I think I'll reread this journal if I can't write the obituary.

February 27
The final class, Sheila Scott is absent a second time.
Later in the day I find her journal in my intramural mailbox with a note urging me to read her journal so that I will understand her absence.
Sheila, I do understand, and you have earned full credit for what you have contributed to me and many others. Remember, it is not the quantity that counts but the quality.

and a time to die

"Her emaciated body just lay there," Miss Butler began as tears streamed slowly down her cheeks. "I sat quietly holding her hand. For long periods of time she lay quiet, maybe even dozing off, then she would come to again. She had been so terribly miserable for so many weeks, in such extreme agony as her body wasted away at the onslaught of that devastating disease. Death could be the only end to this, I kept on thinking. But how long will it take? For some reason, she could not die. It is not that she wanted to die, or that I wanted her to. It is just that it was inevitable. We both knew it. But the process was such an agony."

Miss Butler and I co-taught a course on death and dying. Listen as she continues:

"You see, I am one of the new health care workers who help dying patients in hospitals. It is my assignment to personally be available to the dying and their families for whatever need during the final moments of life. I help the hospital personnel respond more humanely, instead of abandoning the dying as they used to do.

"Last week as I was sitting next to Mrs. Murphy, I realized how far we have yet to go until we are capable of handling the dying process civilly. We have so far to go.

"In the midst of all her agony she would say, 'I am such a burden. My husband drives those several hundred miles every week. Then he stays for so long. The children need him at home. The business needs him, but he feels so compelled to be here.'

"Now the part that made it all so dreadful is when she exclaimed, 'It makes me so angry when he keeps on urging me to take my medicine immediately when it is brought. He is pushing me too hard.' To myself, I thought, 'Isn't this exactly Mr. Murphy. He absolutely refuses to accept the fact that she is dying, even now when she is so near death. But he will not admit it. I even believe that she is hanging on because he will not let go. He has to conquer even death.'

"I have seen Mr. Murphy repeatedly during the last several months. He was absolutely sure that she would not die. His favorite expression was, 'We have licked so many obstacles together, and we are going to beat this one, too.' Since she was readmitted three weeks ago he had scarcely left her bedside, as if he could guard her against the uninvited guest, as if his presence should keep death away. He is totally committed to the fact that he can beat death.

"You must understand that Mr. Murphy is no ordinary person. He grew up in poverty and on his own ingenuity became very successful. With the force of his indomitable will he conquered life. So why should he not assume that he could conquer death also? This is how he ran his business, his family, and his marriage. He had never surrendered. He had never let go, and he was not about to do it now—not even to let his wife die.

"You need to understand that he really loved her dearly. That fact no one doubted. At no time has either one shown anything but tenderness toward the other. He showered her and the children with all the good things in life, like he never knew as a child. They all accepted him as he was, and even admired his zest for life. They both knew that their three children, ages fourteen to twenty-two, needed a mother for a while yet. There was a lot of reason for her to live longer.

"I knew all this when I sat with her this day. We both knew that the reason he stayed by her side was that he could not accept the inevitable. Her life was ebbing away. The agony was simply too much to bear. Then the worst part was that no one could talk about it. 'Oh, if these people could only talk to each other before she dies. If only they could say good-bye to each other,' my heart kept on screaming at me.

"After that, I decided to talk again to Mr. Murphy upon his return to Philadelphia. At first he gave me his lecture on the power of determination and then recited the many victories they had won together. But I kept on saying. 'Mr. Murphy! No matter what you have conquered in life, death you will not conquer. It is man's ultimate enemy.' I showed compassion about how much he needed his wife; how much the children needed their mother; how terribly unfair it is for her to die in her late forties.

"Then I returned to my purpose for seeing him. 'She is suffering just terribly. All we are now doing is prolonging her dying process—not prolonging her life—since death is inevitable.'

"With that, he bowed his head and wept as he replied, 'I wanted so much for her to live, but I really knew it's all over.' He said very little more than that as he left to see his wife again.

"I couldn't go to the hospital last night. But on my electronic answering service was a brief message from Mr. Murphy telling me that his wife went into a coma last night and died shortly thereafter and that he would call me in the morning from home. Today I received a long-distance telephone call. He was extremely grateful for all my help, especially that I had made him aware how terribly miserable she was. Then he finally told me that he did manage to say to his wife, 'Have a good journey,' and shortly after that she died. That was his way of letting go and giving her permission to leave."

Miss Butler finally raised her head as if to proclaim a message out of her deep sorrow. "If you students learn only one lesson in this course, I hope it is that if you are ever faced with the dying you will be able to help people let go. This couple's agony is going to stay with me forever. The last week could have been so much better for both of them had he come to terms with death."

A student then asked her very pointedly, "Do you think she would have died sooner had he accepted it?"

"There is that possibility," was Miss Butler's response.

"Then do you honestly believe that he did tell her that he was accepting the fact that she had to die by telling her to have a good journey? And do you think that as a result she sank into a coma that very night and died the next day?"

"I believe so."

"Then you would say that man has some choice over his exact time of death?" she queried.

"I believe that in some instances this is true. There are several studies that show that people die far more frequently immediately after holidays and birthdays than just prior to these events. What else than people choosing the day would cause this?

"My lesson in all this is: Why can't we come to terms with death in such a way that when the end is near we can participate with others in the final moments so as to help bring life to a dignified closure as well as help those who survive live better with the loss?"

Why can't we? Well, we simply have relegated the idea of death so far into the back of our minds, due to fear, that we cannot bring it into our consciousness enough to deal with it. We cannot have dialogue with death. If we could deal with it, we would come to terms with our feelings so that when the inevitable comes some semblance of decency could surround the bed of the dying.

Death with dignity is the theme of a whole new movement in America. Many health care workers, including doctors, nurses, social workers, and aides, are now preparing themselves, like Miss Butler, to help people die with dignity. Even the dying are now organizing to enable each other to make that final phase meaningful. It will require a lot of dialogue with death by many people before a noticeable change will occur in how we deal with the dying.

Some people intuitively know better than the most informed theologian or psychologist. I think this is best illustrated by a local couple in their early sixties. They had lived a quiet, intimate life together, interrupted only recently by a debilitating and very painful illness. When he took a sudden turn for the worse, his wife became very apprehensive. Instinctively she turned to God in pleading intercessory prayer for his recovery. He turned to her when she was finished and asked, "Could you not pray for my recovery any longer? Pray rather that I may go! My life is finished. I do not live well with this disease. The pain is too much for me. I am so tired of living." She did exactly as he asked, and he died immediately.

What a beautiful ceremony!

Could I accept the fact that there is a time to die? For even me?

I have allowed myself that thought a number of times, especially during the many recent encounters with death that I have so deliberately confronted. I just simply put myself, as best I could, in the other's place. What would I feel like if that were me?

On some occasions the gruesome story of a heroic struggle

has overwhelmed me. Then as I leave the bedside I have uttered a gasp of relief that "God, it isn't me!" But then there have been other occasions too.

Several years ago, my mother-in-law lay dying in a local hospital as a result of a sudden massive stroke. Each day she faded farther and farther away. On the fifth day, my wife and I made our usual trip to her bedside. We each took time to be alone with her even though she generally showed no signs of recognizing us. When my turn came, I took my seat beside the bed and took her very tiny hand. There was no response.

After a while I gave her hand a slight squeeze, and she responded with the same signal. I asked her if she knew who I was. She again used the squeeze to tell me she did. Then I said that she had been a good mother-in-law, and I thanked her for giving me her only daughter. She signaled again and a slight smile crossed her lips. After that her face went blank, and I assumed she had fallen asleep. There was no question that her end was near. She could take no food or liquids, and no intravenous feeding had been ordered. At times we moistened her lips and tongue with a wet gauze pad. Otherwise nothing was to any avail.

As I stood back to take what happened to be my final look while she was alive, I observed that tiny figure who weighed only ninety-eight pounds at best and much less by now. "The same as a bag of flour," she used to say. She looked so peaceful, so quiet, so far away. Obviously that is how one's life comes to an end.

But that was far from how she had lived. I can even now visualize her with all of her boundless vitality racing through the day. She began employment after her fiftieth birthday and still put in twenty-five years to earn full retirement with all the benefits. Only a year before she had retired from Daroff and Sons clothing factory—"The makers of Hart, Schaffner, and Marx clothing," she used to declare. She was a remarkable woman!

I could see her coming home from work and immediately

recording the number of "darts" she had sewed that day on her favorite calendar hung in the bathroom—695, 705, and sometimes 750 appeared on a workday. She never took more than a day or two off for sick time. Twenty-five years sewing darts above the back pockets of men's pants at the average rate of 700 a workday makes more than four million darts, and all after fifty years of age.

At that moment a strange sensation overcame me. Life's work can get finished. There is an end to it. It doesn't last forever, and that's a relief to know. The last pair of pants does get laid down.

For me there will be a last class to teach, a last lecture to deliver, a last client to see, and then it will be finished. It feels good to know. I paused long enough to claim that feeling.

My meditation took one more turn. She was so often preoccupied with political or world situations that made her fearful. And that, too, has passed for her, and it will pass for me, too.

I took one final look and then joined my wife in the hall. My first words were, "She is a lucky woman. I envy her."

There was shock in my wife's voice as she exclaimed, "Why? What do you mean?"

No! I am not tired of living, nor do I want to die to get out of our marriage. It has nothing to do with that.

She is lucky, that's my feeling! A life lived to the full— three score and seventeen, seven more than the proverbial lifetime. She had managed her house until a year before. She spent the last year systematically disposing of her property, distributing her many belongings, and settling all her accounts. To the best of her ability, she was at peace with God and man. And then without notice the stroke stopped her and that was all. She did not want to be an invalid, nor ever have to go to a "home." She always functioned at top speed. She had no way of slowing life down gradually. This, I know, is exactly how she wanted it. It was just exactly the right time for her to die. There is a time to die, and this was her time.

And I do envy her! It feels good to have said that because I am now aware that I have begun to make peace with death, and that means I have also begun to make peace with life. I can say, "I am ready. Come, death."

12

the future of death

Through dialogue with death, I have become increasingly concerned that we deal differently with death in the future. As I have counseled grieving persons, spoken with those who knew they were dying, and discussed death and dying with very much alive students, I have made several discoveries which could change and help every person who must face the ultimate enemy.

Let the dying speak to us. Let the dying, like Orville Kelly of Burlington, Iowa, teach the living the value of each moment. The dying have a very important message for the living if we will only stop long enough to hear them deliver it. The thing they know best is that the only way to live life is to begin now—otherwise we never will. We live only now. While we are not diagnosed terminally ill, we dilute our present with as much of the past as we can regurgitate and as much of the future as we can fantasize. All of this we do to avoid the pain of genuinely living now. We need the dying, who have no future that they can count on and whose past will be wiped out shortly, to tell us that we must make today count.

When Orville Kelly, in the midst of a cancerous death and a deep depression, realized that he still had the present, he woke up to a whole new life for himself and for millions more. He was an instant celebrity; all three major networks have filmed him. Many offers came to him from radio stations, he was offered speaking appointments across the nation. A publishing house wants a book on him. He organized a group of dying patients which has since become a model for groups nationwide known as "Make Today Count."

Finding the key to life in death. The idea that the quality of life is related to the acceptance of finiteness and death runs through this book. It also was a continuous aspect of each course on death that I taught. It couldn't be avoided because life and death are so related. Then why not deal with death at any stage in life so as to add new dimensions to living? My hope for the future is that the process will increase and spread until a new quality of life will become universal—a life that will move from temporal concerns to ultimate cares. Death makes man ask, What really counts?

I again wish to use a journal entry to illustrate how one more student discovered a new freedom to live via a dialogue with death.

April 26
Life = Death = Life = Death
First Birth: beginning of life
Death: of infancy
Birth: of childhood
Death: of being mothered
Birth: of adolescence
Death: of searching for self
Birth: of adulthood
Death: of having to prove self
Birth: of acceptance of life and death as one
Final Death: end of search for life's meaning

April 27

Dr. Schmitt: Dealing with my own death has been difficult
for me. Damn difficult. But I have dealt with it—will continue to deal with it every day that is left for me to
live. I will enjoy my life and give more of myself to others.
I will be sensitive and will try to live at no one's expense
but my own. The death and dying course was most meaningful for me. Thank you for the experience. I feel relieved
and less afraid. Can you tell?

April 28

I thought the entry of April 26 would be my last, but
I must continue. My experience of becoming sensitized
to life and what it brings for fulfillment did not end with
that entry. The next morning, after writing in this book
my deepest thoughts, the sunshine was so warm and
loving. It beamed through my bedroom windows. It awakened me at 7 A.M. although it was Saturday. I could not
go back to sleep. I raised my windows to let life in. My
plants danced on the sills. My joy at being alive was
overwhelming. I called three of my friends and awakened
them too, not caring if they cursed me for disturbing
their slumber. My reason, but only an excuse to them, was,
"I called to make sure you don't miss a minute of this
day." One understood, the other two did not. Well! It's
their loss!

My day was full of activity. I stayed outside for most
of it. I visited my parents, a trip long overdue. . . . I just
had a jolly time. I tried to stay awake as long as I could
for sleep on that day would have been a waste of
precious time—life—time! What a beautiful, unforgettable
experience!

What a bringing together of my physical and spiritual life.

My hope for the future is that we will learn from the dying
and from death how to live.

Death education. It is my hope that more and more courses

on death will be offered for anyone who wishes to be more comfortable with the subject and who is ready to experience his own life more deeply. It should be an integral part of any formal educational process—especially part of programs related to philosophy, religion, and literature. For professionals who have to deal with people, the study of death is a must. And finally, for those who actually face the dying person, it should be an absolute requirement that they dialogue with death, and if possible, with their own death until they too are capable of responding to the needs of the dying rather than to their own unmet needs.

We must stop our present behavior toward the dying as was so appropriately voiced by a terminal guest in the classroom. "Our posture toward the dying is—poised to run."

To illustrate what a death education process can do, I include a letter addressed to me—the final entry to a student's journal on death.

Dr. Schmitt:

In evaluating this course, I cannot think of one single improvement to recommend. My learning and emotional growth have been much more than I have been able to put on paper. Each time I reread an entry, I am ready to change it; but I realize that I have gone through the process; so I leave it be.

This has been a wonderful experience. I am very sorry that you will not be available to give this experience to future social work students, as it has been most valuable to me. Thank you very much for the best course I have ever had related to social work.

This is one more person who I am sure will approach the dying, not "poised to run," but resolved to care.

An appropriate farewell. I recently heard of a young mother of two small children who died of cancer. During her final

days she made a tape recording in which she addressed each
of the children in an appropriate message of parting. At that
time they were too young to understand, but some day such
farewell words will convey very meaningfully how much she
cared for them and would have continued to do it in person
had she been able to do so.

Recently I came across an exceptionally fine parting ceremony recorded in an obscure publication. I believe it should
receive wider distribution.

Monday noon the pain was more intense, and Dave said
to her, "I don't think it will be long now, Doris, until you
see Jesus, and you'll get a new body." Her face lit up, "Oh,
Dave, it sounds so exciting—to think that I'll see Jesus soon."

That afternoon she was in excruciating pain, which the
medicine did not faze. The doctors felt there were serious
complications. The dosage of pain medicine was increased.
They consulted her about returning to the hospital. "How
would it help?" she asked. Admittedly, there was so little to
suggest. She answered, "I'd rather stay here, but I'll do whatever you say, Dave." She stayed.

Toward evening she asked her husband to call the
children into the house. It was suppertime, and they sat
down to eat. But she seemed uneasy, and I asked, "Did you
want them to come here first?" "Oh, yes, please, I do," she
responded with a sense of urgency. I left the bedroom while
they all came in, and she spoke special words to them.

When I returned, I moistened her dry mouth and lips,
but had trouble understanding her and told her so. She
answered, "Oh, I'm talking to God." I listened carefully as
she prayed, "Oh, God, You are all-powerful and could heal
my body with a word. I don't understand all about You, but
I'm all Yours. I'm so ready to go or stay. Just do whatever
You want with me—but, oh God, please take away the pain."

Dave and the children surrounded her bed, and he held
her hand. As the pain eased, she fell asleep. Gradually her

breathing became less frequent until the Lord took her home.*

The patriarchs in the Old Testament of the Bible knew that it was important to bid the descendant an appropriate adieu. One of the finest parting rituals is described in Genesis 48 and 49. When Jacob realized that he was failing rapidly, he asked that his twelve sons and some grandchildren come to his bedside. Then he laid his hand on one head after another, blessed each one, and told that son what share of the Promised Land he should inherit. Jacob very confidently could say, "Soon I will die," and then gave explicit instruction on where he wished to be buried. When he finished, he lay back in his bed, breathed his last and died.

A much more unusual account was told to us in one of our classes by an eighty-four-year-old former schoolteacher. Only recently she had become aware that, at her age, she needed to get ready to go. So she made complete preparation including all the legal forms to have her body donated for medical purposes. Then she placed an announcement in the local paper inviting all her former students to her apartment for an "open house." Sixty-one students arrived. To her, this was a fine way of meeting these people "for the last time."

I wonder, when we become more comfortable with death, whether we won't come up with a whole new form of appropriate ritual to say a final farewell. I believe we will live better with the loss if we have at least had a chance to say good-bye.

---

*Mary Liechty Smucker, "The Last Three Weeks," *Voice*, January 1974.

13

death—
an incredible experience

"I have only a few weeks to live. I know that, and I have made peace with both my life and my death."

Her face glowed as she began the conversation about her death. She was at peace, no doubt about that. There was an air of radiance about her, if not even euphoria. But how could this be?

An instant shock wave encircled the room of twenty-five graduate students. I cringed, wondering what was going to happen today. The apprehension on students' faces only exaggerated my concern.

She was black, single, middle age, and dying. That was about all we knew. She was brought to class in a wheelchair from one of the medical floors below by a nurse who shared in the leadership of this seminar. She had a special reason for having this lady come. She said so, but only indicated that it would be obvious once she told her story.

"I feel like I am very close to death. As I look at all of you, I already sense that you are not quite real, as if I have partially left you. I believe I am just on the verge of opening the door to another room, and all of you must stay behind. Only I can go through. I even feel very special.

"When the nurse asked me to come to class, I immediately told her that I didn't want to. I said I didn't want anyone to spoil the feeling that I have. Dying is very personal and very precious. I simply didn't want to throw 'pearls before swine,' as the saying goes. This is my death, I kept thinking. What good will it be to share this experience with others? I did share these feelings with a group of close friends, and they told me that I had really helped them face death in themselves. Then surely I could be of help to this class. It is their urging that made me come. They told me that the way I was experiencing death was so unusual that I simply had to tell as many people as possible. Maybe I could help others die also.

"Let me try to tell you what I feel like. It is as if I am on a mountaintop. It is very quiet and peaceful up here. As I look back over my life, it all makes sense. I can even understand it all with a lot of meaning. One of my psychologist friends told me it is known as a peak-experience. I am certainly on a mountain peak. The future just looks beautiful. I can see it although I can't recognize anything in it. The colors are just gorgeous.

"My fear of coming is that I thought you might destroy my view. This I just can't let happen. I don't want to diminish any part of my experience because I want to leave this life just as I am. I feel a deep inner sense of completeness, of fulfillment.

"Whatever I think about appears to take on extremely positive attributes, the like I never knew before. I contemplated on the fact that I was single and childless and that I will never know what it means to have children. That often bothered me, but not now. It takes on a totally different perspective. How sad it would be if I were leaving a husband and possibly little children who need a mother! But not now—I am going and it feels like that is just the way it was supposed to be.

Doesn't that even make sense to you? It all feels like it is just the way it is supposed to be. And it couldn't be any different.

"I don't think the feeling that I have is unusual. It feels terribly special to me, but I believe a lot of other people have felt it while dying. Maybe I am only different in that I am able to talk about it. At least I am especially aware of it, but then I have always been very aware of myself.

"I should tell you more about myself so that you will understand it better. I was born in the South, where my only brother and sister still live. They are both married and have children. My brother has two grandchildren already. I was the youngest. Our parents died several years ago—they were old. I even have good feelings about their deaths. They came at the right time. They had lived a full life. In our family I was the only one to go on to college and even some graduate work. That is what brought me to Philadelphia where I have lived my adult life. What makes me feel like I have really lived a complete life is that I was successful professionally. When I was ready for a step up, it always seemed to come at the right time. There were always people around me. Making friends was never my problem. I have dozens of close friends.

"If anything makes my dying hard, it is leaving these people. But then again we have all talked about it. That makes it easier. We have been able to say good-bye to each other. They tell me that they never did this before and that it is my attitude that has made it possible. I just can't remember that I have ever been really afraid of death. I have had that gut feeling that it should be as natural as living. I even kid them by telling them that they have only one person to leave, but I have to leave everybody behind, all at once.

"Let me tell you about my sickness. Only six months ago I had this strange swelling on my abdomen. My doctor was immediately alarmed and suggested hospitalization here. Several specialists saw me soon, and before I knew it, I was on my way to surgery. All this is very vague to me. The one thing I do remember is my family doctor arriving on the floor as I came out of the recovery room. I was not fully aware yet, but asked him what was wrong with me. All he said was one word, 'Cancer.' Then he was gone. I needed to ask him a lot of questions, such as exactly what organs were affected. I tried to get some idea as to how serious it was, but no one would give me a straight answer, only statements like, 'You never know the exact course that cancer will take.' 'We will be using chemotherapy and x-ray therapy.' I felt somewhat comforted by those statements.

"After I left the hospital, I made a partial recovery. Gradually I was aware that I had this terrible feeling of helplessness. I didn't become aware of this until one night I had this awful nightmare. It was a grotesque monster that suddenly leaped upon me. Just before it landed, I woke up screaming. After I became fully conscious, I realized that in the dream I had a vague feeling that this creature was nearby, but I didn't let myself know it was there until it suddenly sprang at me. Then I concluded that what is wrong with me is that I am denying what is happening to me. The monster is the cancer, and I am making myself believe the doctors' comforting words which I really knew were not true. Until then I just couldn't do anything with my time. I couldn't think straight. I couldn't make any decisions. It was as if I were waiting for something to happen.

"Immediately after this dream, I called the doctor and told him I had to know how serious my cancer really was. I had to know what my chances were because I had to decide what I was going to do with the life that was left to me. He said he couldn't understand why I needed to know. Besides, no one can say how serious it is. He then told me that I needed to see a psychiatrist. I agreed on the condition that the psychiatrist would get my chart from him and the hospital and that he would be free to share any information that he chose to share. He settled for that. Isn't it sad that he couldn't tell me?

"The psychiatrist was really nice. At first we reviewed my whole life and together concluded that it had been fruitful and complete. I lived a good life. I had achieved far more than any of my relatives, and I even said that death is OK for me. I assured him that I had a very real faith in God and in life after death. For me, the grave is not the end but the beginning. I was taught this from childhood. I have never doubted that.

"Then I finally faced him directly, 'Now tell me exactly what organs are affected and what are my chances.' It was terribly hard for him to say it. He became completely shook up; so I told him over and over again that I was strong enough for any answer as long as it was the truth. I have to know so I know what I have to cope with. How am I going to live the rest of my life? I must know now. The nightmare story helped convince him that I really was ready for it. So he told me that the surgery was not successful, that the cancer had spread to a number of vital organs, that chances were poor. 'That is exactly what I want to know.' He was terribly concerned about me—wondering if I would be all right. I assured him over and over again that I would be. I finally asked him if he would be all right. Then, I believe he realized that he had a bigger problem with it than I did.

"I left the doctor's office feeling perfectly tranquil. I now knew that my time was short and I needed to make it count. As I walked home, everything I looked at became exquisitely beautiful—the sky, flowers, even the rows of houses. Suddenly I realized that I was saying good-bye to everything, even to the things that are so common to all of us. I was grateful to God for all he had given me, and now I was getting ready to return to him all this, including my life. Really, my life was not mine, either; it, too, was a gift, and my time had come to return it. I wasn't responsible any longer. Isn't that a neat idea? I even felt greatly relieved."

Inside myself I exclaimed, "Wow! What a wholesome view on life!" I had never thought of that before—my life a gift! And dying is merely returning what had never been mine. Say, that makes it easier. Maybe dying can be all right. Then I realized that it took a dying person to teach me that lesson. The living don't know that. Then why not listen to the dying? They have a message to give to the living that they only can teach. Why flee from the dying? They can be our educators about living as well as about dying.

By now I was almost too deep in thought to hear what was happening in the room, but our dying philosopher was talking again.

"The following night I again had a dream. Only this was far more real—so real that I am not sure if it was a dream or a vision. I like to think it was a vision from God. At first, all I saw was a soft color of green all around me. Slowly the inner part became lighter colored, but brighter. Then another smaller area turned more like yellowish-green, and the next smaller area a bright yellow. Each change of color was farther and farther away. The whole thing became somewhat like a huge tunnel of color—the farther away, the brighter the color. The yellow turned to gold, then brighter and brighter gold. I couldn't see the end or how bright it finally became—only it was glorious somewhere at the end. Then I felt the sensation that I was floating in the direction of the far end. It was a beautiful sensation. I woke very peacefully. When I opened my eyes, I simply said, 'So that is what death is like. That I can accept!' Since then I feel as if I don't belong in this world any more.

"After this, I told my closest friends who have stood by

me in all this. They thought it was just beautiful and that my interpretation was true. Now they seemed much more comfortable visiting me and talking just anything with me. We even talk about what it will be like to live without me."

A student asked if these friends always talk about it. "Isn't it kind of morbid?"

"No, we don't talk about it always. They, too, do some denying. Like several weeks ago all my close friends were at my apartment, and a few others they brought with them. They had brought food. We had a lot of fun as we ate sitting around on my living-room floor. Everybody was silly, acting up as we laughed and carried on until past midnight. No one ever mentioned my illness. I felt good, so it wasn't that obvious. But I knew that without anyone planning it this was my farewell party.

"After they left, I quietly prayed, 'Thank you, God, for these people, and thank you for their helping me leave.' "

Suddenly she turned on us as she asked, "Why can't we say good-bye to the dying—after all is it forever in this life? Why can't we celebrate such parting? We can do it for every other ending. Why not this one?"

No one responded to that. No one could. Only the dying could be that perceptive!

A student interrupted the unbearable silence by stating, "I really wonder if what you describe is what death is really like. What exactly will the final moment be? And then, what about the immediate moment thereafter?"

One of our guest lecturers in this class, who was perfectly well, said, "Really, we know only about dying and nothing about death—nor will we ever. Even if we ask people like you who are on this journey, you can talk only about living with dying, not about death. Actually, you know no more than we do about death."

Another student chimed in to differ, "You know, I am not so sure we are at the end of our road to learning about dying itself. I saw a television show recently where a physician and a dying man were discussing death. The physician has just finished a book on his experiences with this subject. He says that his observation confirms that of many others who have stood by the dying, that the final moments are always very serene and peaceful. The dying have described their final view of seeing a long dark tunnel that they were entering but seeing a bright light at the far end. Some have felt like they were just drifting away. Others have seen a curtain slowly closing, but it was bright on the other side. I believe that we know no more about the actual dying experience because we have not allowed the dying to talk. We have refused to listen. Now that people are beginning to deal with death as a fact of life, I believe we will soon begin to learn much more about the dying process as well as the actual experience of dying."

At this point, I told the group that I had recently read a newspaper account of a lady in California who was in the hospital recovering from surgery when she suddenly had the sensation that she was departing from her body and drifting toward outer space. From this height she could see her own body and physicians desperately working on it. She told herself that she was dying, but pled with God to let her live. Then she experienced a return journey until she joined her body. She then regained consciousness to discover that she had a massive hemorrhage but a blood transfusion had been successful. If I recall correctly, she described the whole scene as rather pleasant although she greatly regretted to leave her small children.

I, too, believe that if this is actually true there must be many more testimonies available. However, I doubt that people will talk. We have such taboos about death that people who know will not risk, for fear of being labeled weird. Even the famous William Osler said almost a hundred years ago that death is really not to be feared since it is merciful, and that the experience is like falling asleep and then forgetting.

Another student recalled a newspaper account he had read just recently. It stated that the famous Dr. Elizabeth Kübler-Ross, author of the best-seller *On Death and Dying,* has lately observed the same phenomena on patients whose vital organs ceased momentarily but were revitalized. These patients, she said, felt a beautiful peace immediately and did actually observe themselves leaving their bodies behind. The feeling they had was that dying was an incredibly wonderful experience. Some were even angry for having been made to return to life. She says that some of the more religious people say they were actually met by Moses or Jesus. It seems strange, all this, but then she added that even Dr. Kübler-Ross thought it was so unusual that had anyone else said this to her years ago she would have called it ridiculous.

I then turned to our guest and asked, "How sick are you? How long do you expect to live? What will your death be like?"

"I am very sick," she acknowledged. "I was readmitted to this hospital two weeks ago because of internal bleeding. This is serious, that I know. The physicians are now honest with me since they know I already know all about myself, and I make them tell me everything day by day. There is no improvement. No surgery is going to be done since it is useless. I have only a few weeks to live. It simply can't be much longer.

"Before I answer your last question, let me tell you about last week. After returning to the hospital, I became terribly miserable. I had a lot of pain and discomfort. I couldn't sleep. I lay in bed just begging to die. It was just awful.

"Now I have a very good feeling again. I was afraid that it was going to get more miserable until the end. The present sensation is one of wholeness. I feel like I am in touch with the universe. I am part of a great big world. It is much bigger than I am. If I could only describe it to you. It is very difficult to do. All I know is that I am enjoying my life more now than I ever have before when I was well. If I could tell you, you would not fear death like you do. You would tell others it is really all right to die.

"My death will be just like I am now experiencing. I believe my last dream was a part of it. Now it is getting more intense each day. Even now I feel a great sense of oneness with all of you. It will continue—this experience getting more beautiful. Then finally the last step. Then I will be in the next world and be in total union with all existence."

Thank you, death, for conversing with me! I know I still fear you. There is so much that is unknown about you, but you have permitted me to have dialogue with you, which has removed some of the sting. I now know that you are not only the end of life but an integral part of every moment of life.

how to conduct dialogue with death seminars and meetings

There is a need and a continuing demand for workshops, seminars, classes and meetings on death and dying. Far too many people are unfamiliar or uncomfortable with the subject of death, and help is desperately needed to plan and conduct such experiences. My hope is that this book will be an aid in this emerging process.

One of the crucial problems is to make the focus of the seminar clear. The most urgent need for such workshops—helping people personally deal with death—must be met experientially. The workshop, whether it is an all-day affair or a single session, can do exactly that: it can in itself be the vehicle to help an audience confront death.

My experience with workshops on death reveals that most of them avoid this kind of encounter with death. Two methods currently dominate: The first is to keep the workshop only on a rational level, filling the program with death-related issues on which erudite speeches can be made, and then debating the pros and cons under such titles as: "The Politics of Death," "The Implications of Euthanasia," "Toward a New Definition of Death."

A much more subtle process is to create a program that allows no possibility for having an experience with death.

At a national all-day conference on death and dying which I attended several years ago, the entire day was cluttered with workshops, films, and group sessions all pointing to the grand finale banquet at night. The renowned guest speaker, an author of famous textbooks, was then to honor us with his presence. He arrived but the cocktail hour had been too long for him. He had no prepared speech, but rather delighted the audience with typical after-dinner amusement, only in this case it was gallows humor. I could not laugh for I was crying. Here were the nation's death educators, and they could not handle it.

I believe very special programming is needed to avoid this pitfall and, in fact, make the workshop be a real encounter with death.

I use very specific techniques. First, I insist on calling the occasion *Dialogue with Death*. The potential candidate knows immediately that if he wants to dialogue on this subject he is welcome. If he doesn't, then he may stay away.

The brochure or announcement should give an explicit statement of purpose which invites everyone to an experience. One of the brochures stated it as follows:

The primary objectives of the seminar are to help the participants deal with death so they may enrich their own lives, helping others enrich their lives by bringing one's life to a closure rather than have it torn away when the time comes, and helping the dying meet death with dignity. Thus, the seminar will assist the participants to "dialogue with death" by allowing the dying to speak to us, the living; to face one's own death may assist one in living now; the grieving process includes ambivalent emotions which need to be dealt with before one can live for today. The workshop, therefore, will not focus on issues such as "The right to commit suicide" or "How does one define death?"

Included in the program will be the participants' writing entries in their own personal journals in which they will commence their own "Dialogue with Death"; the showing of the film, "Through the Valley of the Shadow," which is a documentary film of a person confronting the final weeks and days of his life."

A suggested program agenda could be the following:

First encounter experience: On many occasions I read chapter 1 of this book aloud. It is an effective opener and also sets the tone that we are going to face death squarely today.

Journal entry: After the encounter experience each participant is asked to begin a death journal. The pads and pencils are supplied. I simply ask each person to begin the entry with "Dear Death," just as they once may have written "Dear Diary." This writing should remain their private property so as to free them to spill out their feelings exactly as they experience them. I suggest that we take approximately ten minutes for this purpose although I simply watch the audience silently until the majority stop writing. Then I proceed with the next encounter, after which time is again allowed for making another journal entry.

A journal encounter: Some audiences need help in knowing what to write in a journal. Sometimes I read all or portions of chapter 3 or chapter 4 since they include actual entries. When teaching the course in a college or university I ask a former student to come to class to read from his journal. This journal then becomes the first confrontation of finiteness.

Films and film strips for encounter: There are more and more films now being produced that do the job of exposing the truth about dying and grieving very effectively. After showing a film I request total silence as everyone then dialogues with death in writing.

Dying or grieving guests: I am impressed how willing the dying or grieving persons are to come to my workshops to serve as resource persons. Almost everyone I have ever asked has come, even against great odds and with extreme difficulty. None have ever accepted remuneration. Death so often feels so meaningless that to come to a session and use the experience to help others adds, at least, that much meaning to it.

I always interview the guests. At first I ask general questions so as to make them comfortable. Then I become more specific, including a precise question about their feeling about dying and eventually being gone. After very good rapport is established, I invite the audience to join in the discussion. If I feel any question is inappropriate I help the guest avoid it.

These guests are really phenomenal resource persons. Journal entries which have been shared with me usually indicate that such confrontation forces the audience to get in touch with their deepest feelings about death.

Informative lectures: When during the course of a workshop I feel that the emotional load is becoming too heavy and people need a break, I give informative lectures on the subject of death. To simply retell Elizabeth Kübler-Ross's stages of the dying process is one possibility. Another is to take chapter 8 and describe the grief process, including the illustration in chapter 7.

Audience discussion: As a whole I keep audience discussion at a minimum. In large groups meaningful participation is very difficult. Often I specifically request one-sentence feeling responses. Participants say things like, "I am drained"; "I feel like I lost a burden today"; "It may seem silly but I am euphoric."

This type of control avoids the pitfalls of opening up the mike to someone in the audience who has never dealt with his mother's death, and now wants to share every detail of it no matter how inappropriate for this occasion.

Small group processing: An excellent method for teaching is to divide the class into small groups of six people, each with a competent leader, to process that week's encounter and journal entry. I found it best to keep the same groups for the entire semester. This can become a real healing experience. *Obituaries and eulogy:* As a final challenge I ask each participant to try to write his own obituary as it would appear in a local newspaper on this day. The final assignment I make is to write a full-length eulogy as one would like it to be delivered at one's funeral. One is included in chapter 4.